How to Meet a Millionaire

DORIS LILLY

How to Meet a Millionaire

WITH DRAWINGS BY
DOROTHY COLE RUDDICK

G. P. Putnam's Sons   New York

COPYRIGHT, 1951, BY DORIS LILLY

All rights reserved. This book, or parts thereof, must not be reproduced in any form without permission. Published on the same day in the Dominion of Canada by Thomas Allen, Ltd., Toronto. Manufactured in the United States of America.

Van Rees Press • New York

CONTENTS

1.	MY EARLY DAYS AND HOLLYWOOD ONES	3
2.	GAY NEW YORK	16
3.	CONSERVATIVE NEW YORK	34
4.	FOREIGN LANDS: VERMONT, CHICAGO, MEXICO	60
5.	I MEET SYBELLA, OR THIRTY-THREE TIMES AROUND THE ETOILE	81
6.	THE RIVIERA IS FOR PENGUINS	110
7.	I ALMOST BECOME A BULLFIGHTER	139
8.	LONE STAR HOME-COMING	168

How to Meet a Millionaire

CHAPTER I

MY EARLY DAYS AND HOLLYWOOD ONES

I GUESS I ALWAYS WANTED TO MEET A MILlionaire. I first remember wanting to meet one when I was going to high school back in Santa Monica, California. I read all about them in the newspaper columns. The rest of the kids I knew got excited when they saw their names among the social notes in the *Santa Monica Daily Outlook*. I got excited over something big, like Constance Bennett suing Jimmie Fidler for three million dollars.

New York, Hollywood, Europe—all seemed wonderful; Santa Monica was no place, and on top of that my own life was just as dull as it could be. While other people were sitting on yachts, smoking cigarettes out of long gold holders, what was I doing? To give you an idea, I was going to Saturday night community dances, for instance. All the girls wore starchy organdy dresses.

They and the boys would clutch each other at arms' length and race madly around the dance floor with their long legs to some fast tune, all the while holding their heads perfectly stiff. This was obviously not sophistication.

High school itself bored me too. I tried to take gym in as many of my class periods as I could; between times I'd rush across the street with my friends to a place called "The Cave" where kids from a junior high school hung out. A lot of my friends thought it was a marvelous thing to mix with the junior high school group. I didn't.

There wasn't much else going on except the sororities. There was one called the Candysticks and another called the Alphadons. The Candysticks were snooty, and the Alphadons looked down even on the Candysticks. The sorority girls pretty much ran any gay life there was. If you were in one, fine; if you weren't in a sorority, well, you were out on your fanny. I wasn't in one, and I wasn't out on my fanny either, because I just didn't care. I had a good time. Finally I graduated from high school with honors. The honor being, as I often said, that I graduated.

After that I went to a big southern California college, as my mother wanted me to so much and as I thought things might be more interesting there. They weren't, though I did the things that girls were supposed to do. I bought myself some cashmere sweaters, some good-looking scarves, marched in the parades before football games, went out a lot, and tried to be nice and enjoy myself; I couldn't. The men were village idiots with white teeth, crew cuts, and a bottle of gin to be downed

Saturday night. There was one beach called "Muscle Beach." That was where the boys went to tense their muscles, and play volleyball, another way of tensing their muscles. People held wienie roasts and considered them very social. Things were not interesting; they did get dangerous. The driving was fierce—trees, cars, people being smashed right and left. Not to mention what happened to most of the girls. For a time I thought, If I'm going to be killed or raped, I'm going down fighting. Then I thought, If this is the gay young life, I'm crazy. So I left after a year of it.

When I look back on it now, that college seems to me like a broken-down road company performance of a big musical comedy. Just generally, and the way people there were always bursting into song. They would sing parodies of their college songs and then they and everyone listening would laugh a lot.

Well, I felt a little at loose ends then. I wasn't getting any nearer to meeting a millionaire, or a friend of a millionaire, or anyone who'd even seen something of a millionaire, and there didn't seem to be any way of doing any of those things at the moment. It was wartime; I figured I would let things drift for a while in a patriotic way, and got myself a job in a local aircraft factory, working on the graveyard shift. It was the graveyard shift for two reasons: one was that I'd make more money, and the other was that I wouldn't have to get up in the morning. All my life I've hated getting up in the morning; it makes me sick to my stomach.

I still went out a lot; at the stroke of midnight, though, I'd rush home, change into slacks, tie a scarf around my head, grab my badge, and have the guy I was with that evening drive me out to the plant. The first thing I'd hear was always the jackhammer which sounded like someone had put a bomb under the Waldorf and the whole thing was falling down. The work wasn't too hard (I was a dispatcher), and I liked it pretty well. Sometimes people came out to entertain us: you know, someone would play the piano, someone else would do a time step, and for this they would be able to keep out of both the army and defense work too. A lot was going on in that factory besides defense work, let me tell you; no one missed a trick, otherwise or commercially. They had mobile unit shops that used to get the defense workers leaving, before they could even climb into their cars. The plant's big moment came when it was rumored, falsely, that Mickey Rooney was coming to work there.

It was a novelty for a while, but after six months the thing got to be hectic, got to be a strain. Besides the noise and the wisecracks, the same crazy driving went on that went on in college. The road out of the factory was like Indianapolis Speedway; when you got home you felt, in every way, as if you'd been through a wind tunnel.

Besides, it reminded me of high school too much. At the plant, again, I'd keep going across the street to get coffee and something to eat. The only place to go was a terrible joint; I felt like a crumb going in there in my slacks and fur coat. People used to stare at me, but I only did it to keep warm.

When I left that defense plant, that's when I decided that waiting for luck to come my way hadn't worked. It was time for me to go out after luck; I moved to Hollywood. Hollywood was right nearby. Furthermore, it's always been my contention that every girl should have a fling at the movies and a mink coat, particularly the former, which I thought would lead to the latter. And if I was in movies, I would meet quite a few millionaires. That's what I figured, and how wrong I was.

How I got into pictures was this way: I was in a big Hollywood drugstore that sold everything from sleeping pills to toupees, minding my own business, drinking a Coca-Cola, and playing the pinball machine, when I looked over at the next pinball machine, and saw a familiar face. "Where have I seen him before?" I wondered to myself and gave it no more thought.

The next day I was in the drugstore doing the same thing; I looked over and there he was again. I realized then that we had been playing neighboring pinball machines for some time. We introduced ourselves and he said to me "How would you like to be in pictures?"

"Now that's *real* original," I thought to myself, "*real* original. Maybe next he'll break into the black bottom and shout 'Twenty-three skidoo, baby, my wife's gone to the country, hooray, hooray!'" We sparred a little verbally, but he seemed pretty genuine after all. As it turned out, he was not a phony, but an assistant casting director, and I turned out, after a short spell, to be a Hollywood starlet with a role in *The Story of Doctor Wassell*.

That's when I first started to feel myself coming close to the millionaires. I realized that I'd have to be patient, go through the starlet routine first; then everything would be fun.

The starlet routine starts by you getting a contract. Everyone has contracts; human beings have contracts, dogs too, as well as horses, birds sometimes. Then a voice test, a screen test, and an analysis of your face and hairdo. The formula for fixing you up is pretty simple; they won't let you stay the way you are. If you're blonde they want you brunette, if you're from the country they want sophistication, if you're English they want to turn you into a tamale type. Just wait, one day we'll hear that some poor tall girl has had her legs chopped off at the knees. This is followed by the capping of the teeth. It makes utterly no difference if your own teeth are so regular they resemble dentures—they've got to be capped! This means you have them filed about half way down and fitted with porcelain jackets. I had heard it was so painful that I got out of it. As for the hairdo, there are three choices. One is to have the hair resting on top of the head in fat sausage rolls, the second is to have it down with as many lacquered ringlets as possible per square inch (in this case the inch is really square), and the third is to wash the hair and leave it absolutely untouched or wild. If you look closely at a still of some girl with her hair flowing very freely you will notice that the ends are somewhat frayed due to her having had it up and down, straight and curly, so many times.

I proceeded to work in the picture. I got up at five thirty in the morning (you may be sure that I was sick to my stomach), was on the set by six, spent the whole day doing nothing except catching a series of colds. Those sound stages are awfully drafty. Some of *The Story of Doctor Wassell* was played in Java; I went out and bought Dutch newspapers to get myself in the mood; nothing helped as I had received a setback. The censors had taken out half my part, leaving a remainder of only one line. I couldn't throw myself into the work with my old gusto after that happened.

In my effort to be co-operative I went into a big scene of action, a fighting scene, as an extra. Things were going fine until someone accidentally dropped a life preserver on my head, thereby stunning me. They insisted on taking me away in an ambulance though I wasn't seriously hurt, merely suffering from shock.

I could take all this philosophically; it was the outside events that got me down. When you're a starlet you have to go out, be seen around town in night clubs with young actors, who are trying to get a break in movies themselves. I said to myself, "Maybe they aren't millionaires, but, Doris, at least you'll be having some gay evenings." Not at all. We never went out to dinner. The man of the evening and I would go to some night club, trot around the dance floor, our best profiles turned hopefully in the direction of the photographers. When the picture had been taken, home we would go. While at the night club we drank Pepsi-Cola, and the waiter would make a ritual out of putting another ice cube in it. In my wildest dreams, I could never have imagined the cheapness of it all.

You may wonder, "If the men were cheap, weren't they at least interesting or attractive?" My answer would have to be no. All those young actors wore enough padding in their suits to insulate a Barnum & Bailey circus tent. Their jaws were not a little dark from shaving, but their eyebrows were, where they had plucked them. Their hair was never cut till it was curling over their collars, and then it was trimmed so it still curled over some.

Conversationally, it was nothing but agony, agony, all the time. If an actor isn't working, he pretends he is. "Hard day at the studio" is one line. Others are "Shopping for a script" or "Going to New York to shop for a show." Often they grew beards to give people the idea they were working in a costume picture. For a while all of them wore beards; their line was "I'm testing for the role of Jesus Christ in *The Robe*."

Needless to say, more than 90 per cent of these creeps never got anywhere. I don't know where they go. Some sell yard goods in Hunt & Winterbotham's; some turn to ceramics; but most of them like the song says, "never die, they merely fade away."

It all looks grand on the surface though; the gossip columns printed my doings, I got to know lots of Hollywood people, and I was a starlet. Someone once asked me what it took to be a starlet. The answer is, if you have a head, legs, and an Adrian suit, then you're in business.

I was in business all right: I got to know the top actors and the millionaires who were sometimes supposed to be the same people. You may wonder how I can write this so casually: hadn't I wanted to do just this? Yes, I had, but in Hollywood the whole thing turned out to be a gigantic fraud.

Forgive me, but there are no millionaires in Hollywood. If there should be a stray he's in for a visit from India, Baghdad, or Pasadena, and most likely checks right out again. Maybe there are some who have a million or so; they don't spend it, so what's the use? I will say right now that my definition of a millionaire is a man who's got it and spends it.

The trouble with me was that I let appearances fool me. I saw Cadillacs, large houses, and assumed that meant money was being spent right and left on gaiety. I soon found out that everyone in Hollywood has a Cadillac, paid for, half paid for, or on loan. (To show you how much the Cadillac is like home to Hollywood people: they all wear dark glasses on the street and often in restaurants and night clubs—when they climb into their Cadillacs they take the dark glasses off, just as if they were in their own parlors.) Everyone mildly important has a big house, too. Between taxes, agents, putting up a front, that's about all they have. I'll give you a few examples of their poverty and stinginess.

One millionaire in Hollywood is famous for his tennis parties. And they're fun, too, except after playing tennis all afternoon on wonderful courts, surrounded by beautiful grounds and ten servants, it comes as a surprise to find that the refreshments are peanut butter sandwiches served on paper plates. There's only one other hitch; you have to bring your own tennis balls. I was very popular there; my host named a tennis ball after me.

Another time I was having dinner in Palm Springs

with a man who got five hundred thousand dollars a picture. We were each drinking a Martini and had almost finished them. There was just a little bit of cocktail left in the bottom of the glasses when he asked me to dance. We danced. When we got back to the table, the waiter had taken them away, thinking we had finished. Well, you should have seen that millionaire's face when he saw that the Martinis were gone. It became contorted with rage and twisted into a dozen ugly shapes. He screamed and howled until the management gave us two fresh Martinis—for free, need I add?

They gave you cigarette lighters, gold or silver, then when you refused to be seduced took them back for initialing, and you never saw them again. What it boils down to is that the generous Hollywood millionaire is the one who takes you out to dinner without making a scene.

I defy anyone to get any money whatsoever out of them. Cash, no; present, no; parties, no. Just no, no, no. All you got out of them is talk. And what talk. It's the picture they were just in, or the picture they're making, or the picture they're going to make. And all they do is knock other people. "So-and-so was awful in such-and-such, I could have done it better." "Isn't what's-his-name looking old?" Knocking all the time. They're great knockers in Hollywood.

There was once that one of those millionaires did act quite high-toned and openhanded. As it was one of the most humiliating days of my life, I will describe the sequence of events.

The guy had invited me to go swimming and have

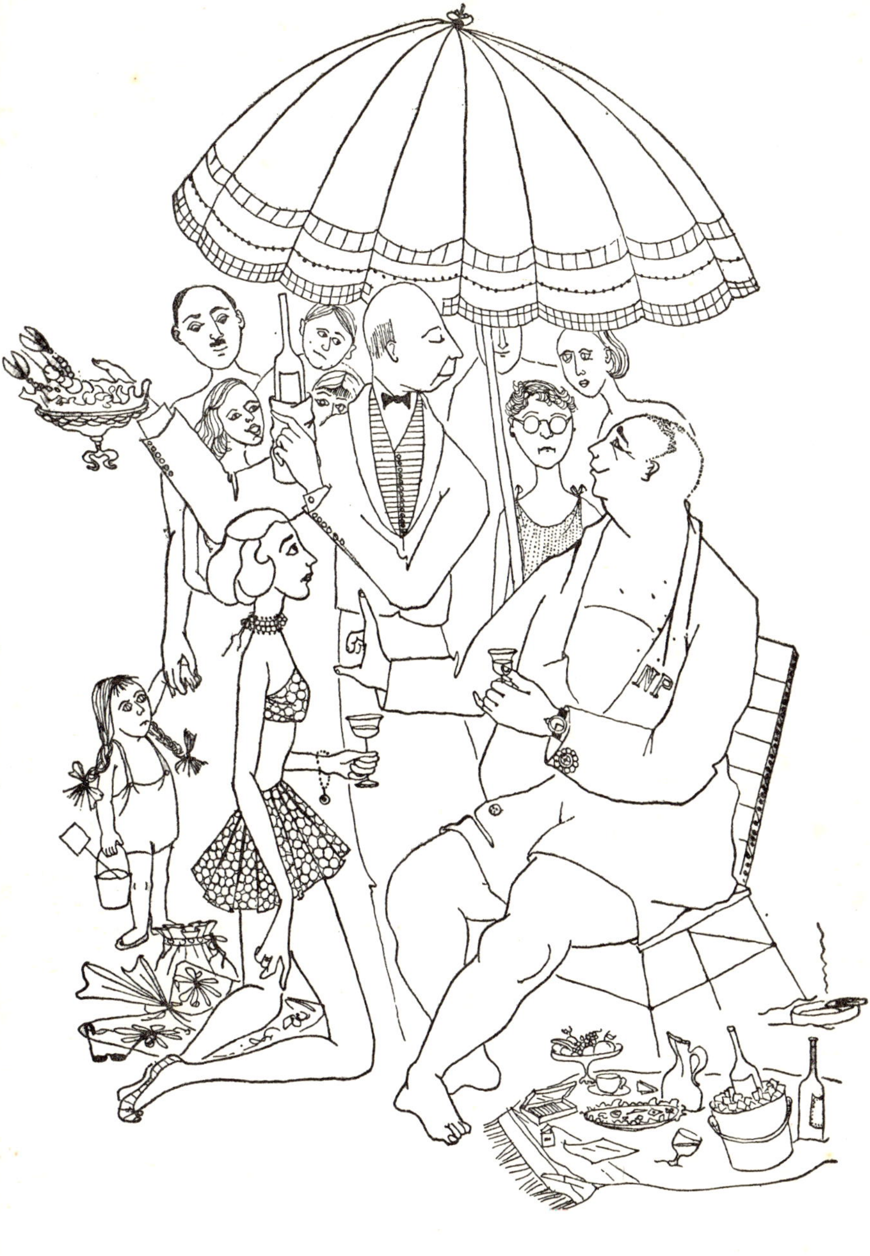
NP

lunch with him at the beach. I accepted. At noon he drove up to get me in a limousine complete with chauffeur, footman, lunch basket, beach chairs, and an enormous ugly mastiff. We drove to a pretty, public beach some distance from Los Angeles. The humiliation started when the footman in full uniform spread the towels out on the sand set up the chairs and the umbrellas. A few people stared. It was nothing compared with what was to follow. We went for a swim, sunned, and the millionaire patted the mastiff who was tied to the leg of his beach chair. He then asked me if I'd like lunch. I said yes, little knowing. Back came the footman with a hamper. He served lunch: *pâté de foie gras,* caviar, chicken, lobster, shrimp, poured the champagne into glasses, and stood all lunch to keep serving the wine. The crowd had trebled by the time he had started the whole thing. When he had finished a wide ring of people was around us, talking like we were something in a zoo. "Who are they?" "Are they crazy?" "Tell me what they're eating, Marie, I can't see them from back here." This was also nothing; just when we were finishing lunch the mastiff caught sight of another dog way down the beach and lunged for him. The dog must have dragged that millionaire and his chair almost all the way down to the water before the footman caught him, amidst the loud applause from something like nine hundred people. This is Hollywood generosity.

It was all a nightmare, a terrible dream. I found out one thing, however: I noticed that the actors were nervous about their agents, the agents nervous about studio producers, the producers about the chiefs of production, the chiefs of production about the studio heads, the studio heads about the banking firms in New York who financed the studios. By this time I was nervous too. So I cut through the red tape, and went to the natural habitat of the millionaire, New York. I figured to myself, why be nervous with somebody twelve times removed? Go to the City, Doris, and be nervous right up at the source.

CHAPTER 2

GAY NEW YORK

I WAS TOO EXCITED TO BE NERVOUS THE boiling day in the dead of summer when my plane landed at LaGuardia Field. I climbed into the airplane company's limousine and told the driver to take me to the one hotel I knew of in New York—I'll call it the Elchester-Flores. The Elchester-Flores was to me a combination of the Taj Mahal and Buckingham Palace, and I could just see myself inside it, with a famous chef preparing me rich, soft food—the kind that turns your gums into ruins. When I said the name, I wondered why the other passengers didn't register more envy; I guessed that they were merely hiding it as best they could.

The driver pulled up in front of a huge imposing place, and I got out, just shaking. Little did I know it was the back end of the Elchester-Flores, not the front at all. I headed for the first door I could see, revolved it, and found myself in a branch of the Chase National

Bank. I revolved right out of there again and finally got to the hotel lobby and the desk clerk.

"I want a suite, please," I said to him. Mind you, it was still wartime, and that place was jammed with people who looked terribly important. He looked at me as though he thought I'd been living in a cave for some time and hadn't heard what was going on.

"We haven't got a suite, miss," he answered through his nose. I just stood there. "But we might have a single room," he finally said. As I had about seven dollars in my purse, this was exactly what I'd wanted all along. I registered right away. I felt that the desk clerk knew what the real situation was all the time, but I gave him a parting shot.

"Please have my trunks sent up when they arrive from Hollywood," I told him.

I handed my only suitcase to the bellboy, and we shot up to my room. I tipped him a dollar just to show them what was what.

There I was, in my room; it was one of their ordinary rooms, and I had six dollars to my name, but to me it was paradise.

I got right on the phone and called some people I knew. None of them were in—not even Junie, my best friend back in California, who'd come to New York a few months before I had. I didn't realize then that people got into New York every day of the week and New Yorkers didn't get a bit excited.

Finally I remembered the name of a man a friend of mine in Hollywood had told me to look up. The man was a producer; he had a musical on Broadway, and my friend had told me the producer would get me a job as a show girl if I wanted to be one. My head was filled with legends of Gladys Glad and Billie Dove; I didn't know that show girls aren't what they used to be. I called the producer—Jack, his name was—and he immediately asked me to have dinner with him. (He was always delighted to meet a new recruit. Word has it he's still up and out at dawn, meeting the Greyhound buses, his tiny eyes peeled for new arrivals.)

In my ignorance I was out of my head with joy. He picked me up at the hotel, and we went to dinner at a place I now know to be one of New York's grisliest—a hot spot for drummers where everything, and I mean the drinks too, is strictly plastic. It couldn't have been worse, but that night I loved it. And then he took me backstage to see his show; saucers were pin points compared to my eyes—that is, until I saw the show girls: bleached hair, knotty legs, some dressed, mostly naked. I thought, Deliver me from this! I didn't know what to do. I'd already told him that I would be in his show. When it came down to the draw, it was only an inspiration that saved me. I got out of the whole thing by saying that I was subject to severe colds and would have to have lots of shots and treatments before I could appear, and so I never did. It was almost the closest escape of my life. I might still be tramping the boards if I had accepted.

My life for a while was pretty quiet after that evening. I got hold of Junie; she was in the same boat I was, not knowing many people (at that time we'd only met a few—broken-down foreigners mostly), and worried about money. This last bothered me. The allowance I got from my family didn't go far, and the Elchester-Flores was after me in a polite way for my rent. I couldn't blame them there—I hadn't paid a cent since the day I moved in. The monotony was broken by a windfall. It was an invitation, actually, to go to the races with about the only rich man I knew in town. I thought the racetrack was a right fine place to go. After all, if I didn't have money at least I'd be where I was near it.

On the way out, as we were driving along in this man's car, an embarrassing thought came into my mind and wouldn't go away. I thought and thought, and I just had to ask him the question finally. I said, "When we get out to the races, do I buy my own tickets to bet on the horses or do you? I truly don't know." I truly didn't.

He turned to me and said, "Doris, I admire your honesty, and I tell you what I'll do. I'll loan you six hundred dollars—that's a hundred dollars a race. If you win, you can pay me back right away. If you lose, you can pay me back later on. I have confidence in you, and a girl as honest as you will make money, I know it."

I had no qualms about taking the money; it was a business arrangement, and I was too broke to be overly fussy. The upshot of it was that I bet on every race, and I won, fortunately. I won two thousand dollars. I paid him back then and there, and when I got back to the hotel, I paid them too, telling them my check from the studio had come through.

I called Junie right away, of course. She had had a

windfall herself. One of those moth-eaten dukes or counts or somethings had found her an apartment, big enough for both of us. It was then we decided we would move in and share the place.

Since Junie and I shared lots of escapades as well as an apartment, I'll try to describe her now. I'm tall, blonde, brown eyed (a direct descendant of Leif Ericson, and proud of it), and kind of ominous looking. When people see me coming, they say, "Scatter, and try to make it look like a party." Junie, on the other hand, though she has brown eyes like mine, is dark, small, a petite type, and innocent looking. People gasp at the things she says. Her wit knows no moral bounds —anything for a laugh, and what fun she is! Men adore her; she's supposed to have been engaged as many times as I've supposed to have been, but she's always turning them down for one reason or another. Even when we were first in New York, I used to think what a contrast Junie was to the world she moved in. This world was glitter and ballyhoo, but little Junie was as real as pumpkin pie and Thanksgiving.

Our apartment was in a remodeled brownstone house; it wasn't grand, but we loved the place. "Wasn't grand," I say. Actually, it was awful. Pitch black, because of no side windows; so old that when you cleaned, all that happened was that the dirt got scrubbed in more firmly; sunken beds; chairs with legs off; lamps that didn't work, weren't even wired to work; and small—just a living room, bedroom, kitchen, and bath, and a tiny spare room we called the den. The den had a chair in it, and a midget guest bed, topped with a horsehair mat-

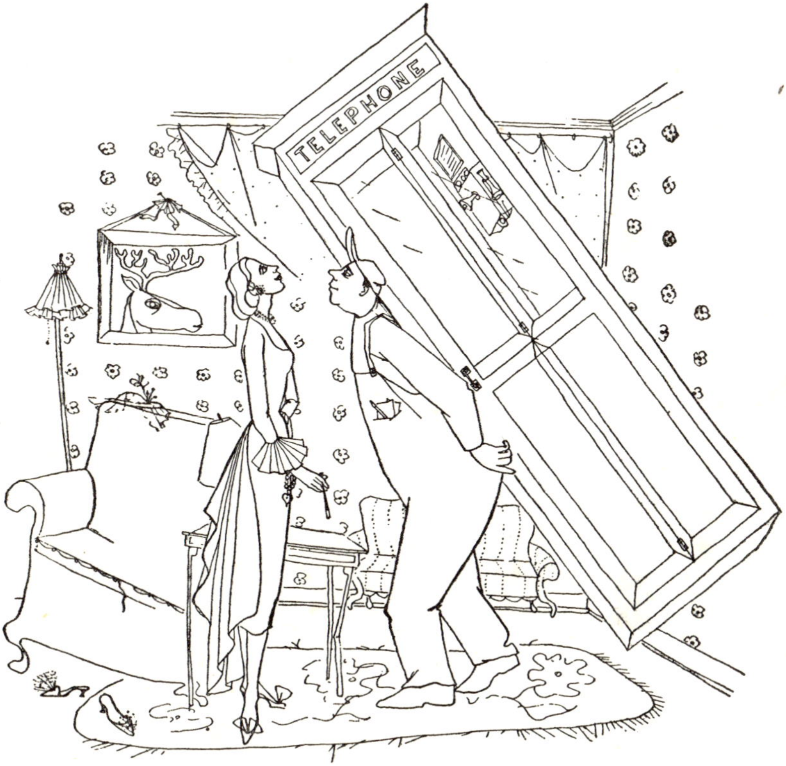
TELEPHONE

tress that sounded like you were bringing in the harvest when you turned over in it.

Junie and I used to sit for hours drinking coffee and planning how we were going to decorate the apartment. Two very bad water colors of deer heads, bought at a sale, was as far as we ever got with the project. We both liked it the way it was.

There was one big problem we hadn't settled—the telephone. We didn't have one. At that time you had to have a priority or a baby to get one; we didn't have and weren't expecting either, so I fell on a unique idea. Pay station phones weren't on the priority list. I called the telephone company and told them we would be glad to take all the calls for the other tenants if they would install a pay station phone on the landing.

I was all ready for the service man when he arrived. He stood there, ready to break open the hallway wall to put the phone in, and I stood there, in a pretty gown, saying, "It would be terribly nice to have the instrument in the den, so much more convenient, with the cold weather coming and all."

He thought it over for twenty seconds, and agreed.

I watched him put it in, so he wouldn't change his mind, and told him that the little enclosure that comes with this type instrument, though suitable for Grand Central Station, wasn't needed here. I also tried to turn down the signs with the pretty girl reminding you to "Please wait for the dial tone" and "Please give your party time to answer."

"They are nicely framed," he pointed out, impressed by the drabness of the den. I gave in.

As soon as we got settled, we started to go out a lot. Junie and I had met more people at cocktail parties and were beginning our whirl, which hasn't stopped yet.

New York has lots of different kinds of people in it, lots of different parties, night clubs, and atmosphere. I have noticed once you meet one of a certain kind of person, you meet his friends who are like him, and you start going out with groups.

When I was first in New York, for instance, I used to see a lot of sports writers, or what I call the Natty Set. Sports writers are a special kind of people, believe me. They remind me of a bunch of gregarious fish in sports coats. They wear tweeds, dark shirts, and light ties, and purposely crush their hats out of shape. They think it's clever to live in the crummiest of all possible West Side hotels; "let the mountain come to Mohammed" is their theory. Best of all they love to talk. Most of them get up late, write a column, and spend the rest of the day talking to their friends about the column. They talk about averages—all the time averages—who pitched what, who batted which, what guy hit the other guy most often— not just to their buddies, but to the girls they take out too. Why, the one that took me out used to sit in a restaurant with his eyes riveted on the door, waiting for someone to come in he could talk averages with. When some friend did come in, this sports writer would yell and scream and wave his arms till the guy came over, and then the talking would start. If there wasn't anyone else who would listen, he would buttonhole the waiter.

I know the wife of one of them. She's never been

known to finish a sentence. Another girl I know eloped with a sports writer. The best man was a sports writer too. All the way to the town where the marriage was going to take place, the groom and the best man talked about Bob Feller till the moment the altar was in sight. All the way back they talked about Joe DiMaggio. My own experiences were the same. One night another girl and I thought we'd drop into a restaurant, latch onto some beef stew, and go to a movie. While we were eating, one of these sports writers spotted us. He rushed over, sat down at the table without being invited, and proceeded to talk for an hour and a half without pause. I couldn't even break away, and when *I* can't break away, that's going some. The other girl, who is not too bright mentally and is liable to go to sleep if things are dull, tried to snap herself out of a light doze by telling one story—one little story. Would you believe it, the few minutes she was telling it that sports writer turned all the way around in his chair and talked to someone else till she had finished it? And they have no regard that they might be boring you; nothing you can say to them is of interest, but what they say to you is just breath-taking. You'd think they were reading you a transcript of Lincoln's "Gettysburg Address." Averages! What I say is, who cares? Who knows? Who fought last night? Maybe it was a new Dempsey, but with most girls, including me, who cares? What is it all anyhow?

But they sure entertain each other. When they get together it's a case of you listen to me, I'll listen to you. They have special expressions like, "Do you hear me good?" which they slay each other with. There's another favorite—"You look like who struck John," the exact meaning of which I don't understand to this day. Oh, yes, that noise you hear isn't a gale blowing up—it's the sports writers talking together. There must have been a fight last night.

Another gabby group, in a different way, is the New York actor group. I went to dinner at the home of one actor; during the meal he regaled me by reading a whole play aloud, acting out every one of the parts in different voices. After dinner he took a book down from the shelf and started to read it aloud. About a quarter of the way through he closed it, marked the place, and remarked that he'd save the rest for the next time. There was no next time.

New York actors have other angles, some of them odd. Like one who was a great beau of mine for a while—he took me out, wined me, dined me, just thought I was grand. But he never sent me any tokens, no notes, no "just called you up" phoning, no flowers. I said to him, "Why is this—no notes, no phones, no flowers?"

He drew himself up, eyed me, and answered, "Doris, dear, I always *live* the role I'm acting, and right now it's not that kind of fellow. Try to catch me sometime when I'm playing Beau Brummel."

Actors love to show off, and that's it. They love slightly second-rate night clubs where Celebrity Nights are a feature. Somehow they always manage to drop in, purely by chance, you understand, on Celebrity Night. An actor will sit there, looking as if he's trying to hide, until the master of ceremonies sees him and shouts out,

"Why, there's that fine performer, Johnny Glockenspiel! Come on up here, Johnny."

Johnny then smiles modestly and says confidentially to you, "I don't really want to do this, but my public, you know." Actually he's just filled with happiness because his name has been hollered out across a roomful of drunks. He goes on, all right, and once he's on, there's only one problem—to get him off again. That's what masters of ceremonies are for, I've decided.

Wherever there are actors, the theater intellectuals are not far behind—just as talkative, but not as amiable. I remember a theater intellectual. The nicest thing about him was his voice, which was deep and soothing. He used it for droning on; I didn't care too much, its quality was so pleasant. He lived in a studio apartment —a huge place, and unclean. The maid was not allowed to throw away any papers, just in case he had written down an important thought on one of them. Some of the papers dated back to the Flood from the looks of them. The clutter was increased by a rare species of South American monkey smuggled into this country by the intellectual. (The monkey was forbidden in the United States because it spread disease.) You never knew when he (the monkey, I mean) would clamber up on your head and start tearing you hair out. In this setting the intellectual brooded and read heavy books— economy, politics, histories of the theater. In the evenings he would go to parties and sneer. He always went to them, and he always sneered. He was the kind of person who would like to get up on a gigantic balcony and spit on the world.

I also went around with a successful New York comedian for a time. Now, with comedians I learned that you've got to be very, very careful because things with them are specially special. The comedians themselves are nice guys, and, mostly speaking, don't have rivalries or feuds; it's their followers, the worshipers, that cause the trouble. It goes like this: you're sitting in a restaurant with a comedian; but you two are not alone, oh, no, his followers are there. What these characters do I never quite figured out. Maybe they're bookies, touts—who knows? Anyway, their main purpose in life is to find a comedian. They find him; they think he's wonderful; they spend their time following him around, listening to him and laughing and laughing at what he says. They also consider it their duty to hate every other comedian in the world but their favorite. So you're sitting in this restaurant, and another comedian comes in. Innocently you say, "Isn't that So-and-so coming in the door? I saw him in Such-and-such, and I thought he was a howl." There's an awful silence, and one of the followers turns and favors you with a long, long look. Then he says, slowly and amazed, "What, you like that schmo? *That* schmo? Why, I've been on this street twenty-five years, and I never saw anything *so* low, so awful," and on and on. Which starts a fight and makes for hard feelings. My advice is, when you're out with a comedian and followers, don't give an opinion. Say as little as possible about anything, and nothing about other jokesters, and you'll stay out of trouble.

I always feel sorry for the comedians themselves; once a man is a comedian, he's got to be funny all the time without letup. A comedian can't walk into a place and say, "Hello, it's a nice day, isn't it, I feel fine." No, he's got to walk in and fall flat on his face. He can't say, "Pretty cold out, it seems to me," instead he's got to say, "It's *so* cold out that I didn't use my alarm this morning—I woke up because the birds were coughing so hard outside my window." Ha, ha. After that, one of the worshipers will say proudly, "That's my boy who said that, *that's* my boy." When the comedian leaves, it's not good-by. Too plain. No, it's "I leave you with two words—penicillin." It gets to the pitch where if the poor guy says, "Has anyone got a light?" four people fall down laughing. I never could figure out what makes the followers act the way they do. I guess they're just the kind of mentality of the person who slams you in the ribs and whispers, "Hey, there's Bob Hope over there!" To which you answer, "Yes, I saw him." Then he says, "*Hey*, that's *Bob Hope!*" "Yes," you say again, "that's nice." To which he says, "HEY, THAT'S BOB HOPE OVER THERE." I don't get it.

There's still another type of person in New York you've got to watch out for: you've got to watch out for the simple reason you can't recognize him. I remember I met a man at a party and thought he was most attractive. He was well dressed, mild spoken, and polite; just a quiet, nice guy. I asked someone what he did. When they told me, I almost had a heart attack. He was a member of the Orange Gang in the Middle West, which had the habit of pouring gasoline over its victims, then setting them on fire, or rolling them up in concrete, and dropping them in a river. Take my word for it, you never would have known it, either. The old-fashioned idea of a gangster—tough, mean, a cigar hanging out of his mouth, hat pulled down, coat collar pulled up—is out. The modern mobster is suave, gentle. No armored car for him. Generally he's interested in real estate, or he has a perfume business. There's no way of telling him from a businessman—no way at all, so a girl just has to be extra cautious.

All these characters hang out in pretty much the same kind of place; a big West Side night club. There are lots of kinds of night clubs in this city, but a big West Side night club is something special.

It really is big, to begin with, and dark and decorated with lots of murals, mirrors, and shining chrome-type trim. Usually there's lots of music, show girls, comedians, a lot of entertainment. In some of them, all that would have to happen is for J. Edgar Hoover to walk in and the place would clear out in two seconds. Most of the people that go to them, though, are respectable people just out to enjoy themselves.

The women who go to them look as if they have a race on to see who can get the most sequins on their dresses. Most of them have sequins, but if you want to go the limit, it's beading. They carry beaded bags; it used to be a mark of chic until some smart guy started to make them for about five dollars apiece, and then the women with two-hundred-dollar ones felt not too happy. Their shoes have two classes of necessary equipment—ankle straps and platforms. They like to have ankle straps *with* ankle straps and platforms so high they look as if they're standing on Pier No. 9. Also, they like to get more sequins or hobnails on the platforms; if not, they'll settle for plain platforms and ankle straps—those they must have. The dresses are skin tight, with wide, sharp, padded shoulders. Their bosoms are hoisted till they rest on the collar bones, the hips look as if they're enclosed in about three girdles—which they usually are.

With jewelry the rule is, don't leave anything at home. Put it all on: rings, bracelets, pins, gold, silver, anything, just so long as it's all there. The rule for hair is, it mustn't look like hair. It's screwed up on the head, then lacquered, sprayed, and Simonized. Put a bone through it and there you'd have a cannibal. It mustn't be the color of hair either. It's got to be something you've never dreamed of before: moonshine blue, head of lettuce green, red with a streak of gray in it, gray with a streak of red in it. The furs are magnificent. In Hollywood people can't afford furs so much. If they do have a coat, it's liable to be lynx-dyed goat; and it may not be good, but believe me, George, it's big. In the West Side night clubs the furs are big, and they're good, and there's lots of them, not only in the club, but at home as well. Like the comedian said at one of those spots, "Flash! Something unprecedented and terrible has happened! A woman just walked in here wearing a cloth coat!" The women love to dance; it sets those sequins shimmering. They dance for hours, never tired, never a hair out of place. Anyway, it would take a team of horses to get one of those hairs out of place.

The men are bland-faced, draped in double-breasted suits. I always imagine them as wearing money belts.

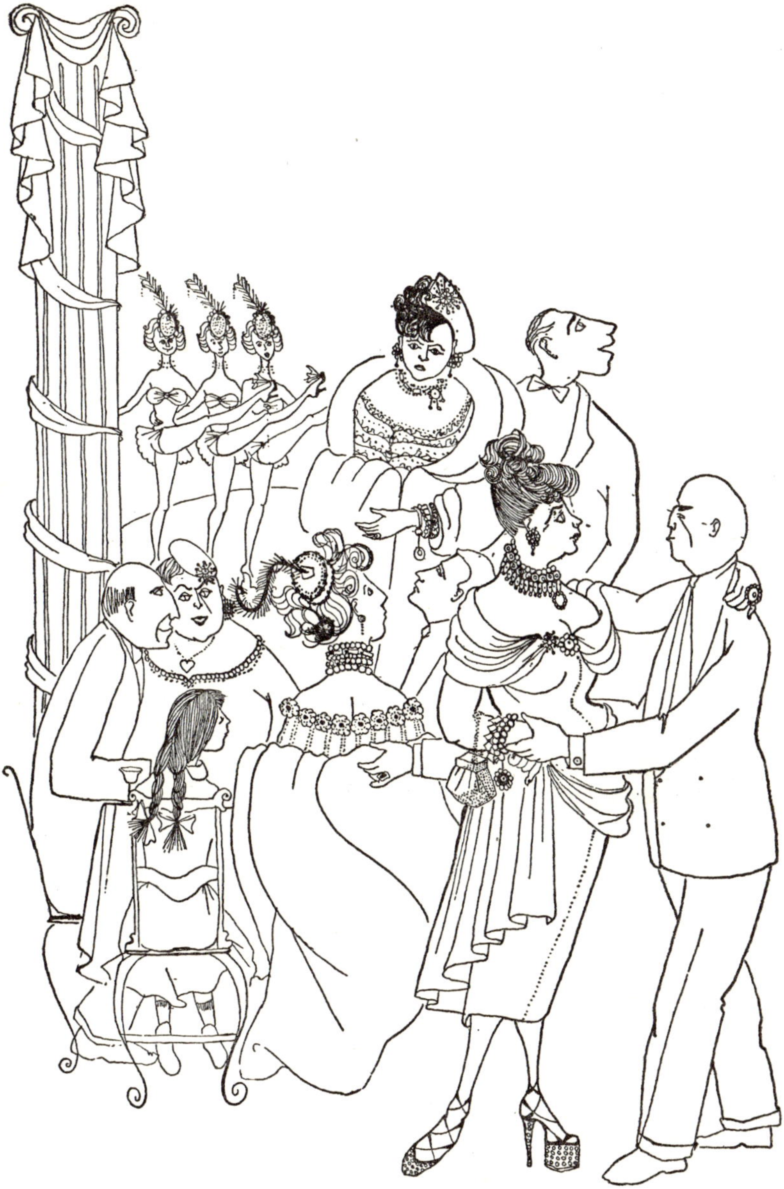

They pride themselves on knowing the entertainers. In the East Side clubs it's knowing the headwaiter that counts; on the West Side it's being chummy with the entertainers. The men say, "Isn't Harry great tonight?" or, "Isn't Sophie in grand form? My friend Soph." All the things you hear about men sitting at ringside tables tweaking the chorus girls is nonsense. If they tweaked a chorus girl, the wife would chop their arm off. Because here the men go out with their wives, which is more than you can say for the East Side spots.

And the children—I almost forgot the children. The parents like their children to realize they know the entertainers; so there the little gnomes sit, spooning their baked Alaska between dirty jokes. The entertainer cries, "I see that This-and-that is here tonight with Junior." Junior makes a note of that, goes back to school the next day, tells the other kids about it, and right away he's a big shot.

These clubs don't care if you're social or not. The management wants to get the people in and out, show them some fun, and get the money. And that's what happens. The people who go to these places are good steady people who spend a lot of money. They tip like mad. They order in job lots: liquor, ice, mixer, and the bottle's on the table. They order, and get, good food, quantity food. They really enjoy themselves. They laugh, they howl, they give it a real dance, a real drink, a real dinner.

Particularly a real dance. They dance and dance and dance—rhumbas mostly, holding each other way off, juggling the shoulders, the legs, the hips; the theory being that the best dancer is the one who can last the longest on his own.

Both Junie and I were having a lot of fun; it was real gay and gaudy. We had gone on like this for quite a time, and could have gone on longer except for four things: Junie met a man who gave fabulous café society cocktail parties; we still had our hearts set on millionaires; there was a fire; and I decided to get charm.

The fire was the immediate cause. We were still living in the pit-type apartment. There was an old woman living across the way who used to make us mad because she had her head out of her window all day long and half the night trying to see into our place. Old Nosey we called her. Well, one night I went to bed, and woke up on the sidewalk with three firemen grinning at me. Junie was there too. What had happened was that the refrigerator had caught fire, had set the whole kitchen ablaze, and the smoke had asphyxiated Junie and me. Snoopy was leaning out as usual and called the fire department. I must say we owe her a debt.

Besides practically ruining the apartment, this fire scared me. It didn't scare Junie; she was fearless. She would go and eat Chilean beans on Tenth Avenue at five in the morning if she felt like it, because she liked Chilean beans and because she knew no fear. Not me. I was frightened. So we moved into a new apartment, and a whole new kind of life.

CHAPTER 3

CONSERVATIVE NEW YORK

OUR NEW APARTMENT, WHILE IT WASN'T the final word in swank, was a big improvement over the Black Hole of New York we'd been living in. It made us think. In fact, the first evening we were settled Junie and I stayed in, drank cokes, played gin rummy, and thought a great deal.

"Doris," she said to me, after we'd been doing this for a couple of hours, "Doris, enough of this. Enough of these sports writers and comedians. Let's start something new."

"I agree with you, Junie," I answered. "But what new, and how?"

"Café society, that's what new," said Junie. "It'll be more exciting. And this cocktail party we're going to Friday. That's how."

"I'm with you on the café society all right," I told her. "But what will the cocktail party do for us? After all, lambie, we've been to a bunch of cocktail parties before. That's how we met these sports writers and people, remember?"

Junie put down her cards. (She was behind, anyway.)

"Doris," she bent forward and looked very serious, "those were parties where people just came and drank cocktails before going out to eat dinner. This is a cocktail *party*. I've only been to a few, but they're different. You'll see."

I was just going to ask her what was so different about them when a great big moth flew out from behind the cushion I was leaning on. Even Junie, fearless as she was, let out a scream, and we both headed for the door, falling all over each other. I got out first, naturally, and didn't stop running until I was halfway down the outside hall. Not until then did I realize I was wearing merely the top of my pajamas. I started to run back into our apartment when I heard voices, a group of people back from a party. I crouched in an angle of the wall, and they didn't see me, though they must have wondered why Junie was standing in the doorway laughing so hard the tears were running down her face. She brought me a robe, and we got the elevator man to catch the moth. So it wasn't till Friday that I found out why the café society cocktail party was so different.

I gave it my attention while waiting for it to happen, though. After a few days, "cocktail party" got to be a golden phrase. It was associated in my mind with wearing a hat, and with those advertisements for "the cocktail dress." In fact, I thought the party and the dress were practically synonymous; I had a vision of a sort of lacy dress with a nude-looking net neckline, worn with elbow-length gloves. In my imagination there was a glass sewed to one glove, and a cigarette in a holder sewed to the other.

By Friday I was in a state almost of frenzy. I got all dressed up and went to the snappy hotel where the party was. My heart was pounding when I heard the voices. I walked in trying to look casual. It was the most horrible fifty seconds of my life. I didn't know a soul; half the room turned and stared at me like I was a worm. They had precedence, they had arrived ten minutes before I had. All I wanted to do was to sit down, though I saw at a glance that the thing to do was stand up and mill around. But I suddenly felt that my dress didn't fit too well in back and that my shoes wouldn't bear very close inspection. I thought quickly, saw where the biggest cluster of people was, wedged my way over to them, and teetered on the edge of a coffee table to make myself a member of the group. It was the best thing I could have done, and it's my advice for an opening move to a girl new to cocktail party going. Get into the unit; if you're not connected with them at least physically, you're out in the cold, cold air.

Well, I settled myself on this coffee table. I still felt nervous but a lot better than I had. I listened and laughed at the jokes and looked at some new arrivals as if *they* were some crumbs fallen from the loaf of life. Some old goat trotted up and started to talk to me. "I didn't catch your name," he said. My face lit up like a Christmas tree, and I told him mine and he told me his. He asked me how long I'd been in New York. I wanted to be witty, catch the ear of some one of the attractive men I'd begun to notice. I was witty all right. "Six months," I snapped right back. Fred Allen couldn't have topped it. And I told him I thought it was deevine when he asked me how I liked it. (I'd just heard someone say "deevine" and thought it was a deevine word.) I loved it madly. Then he asked me if he could get me a drink. I already had one which seemed as big as a house and as bright as a torch. I was terribly conscious of it and of my feet.

I noticed attractive people around me more and more, and I wanted to get to talk to them, but this guy just had me holed in. So I said, "Excuse me for a moment," hoping he'd think I was going to the ladies' room. The room was so jammed that I bumped into some people on my way through it, got into conversation and everything was smooth sailing from then on at that party.

Junie came in and we both talked to the man who was giving the party. He already liked Junie and he liked me too. That was nice, because he was one of the most prominent men in café society, a great party giver, night clubber, and pick-the-check-upper, and a great friend to the girls.

So Junie and I got to going to one cocktail party after another, to almost all the worth-while cocktail parties in town. Actually I'd feel personally injured if there was a cocktail party that I wasn't invited to. I would get in early in the morning from a gay evening, and sleep until it was cocktail time again, get up, go to the party and have canapés for breakfast. I thought I was one of the beats of the pulse and that I was having a hell of a time. Well, I did get around fantastically, got to know practically everyone, and I learned and saw a lot.

When I first went to cocktail parties I had a hard time understanding the other women who went to them. They all talked and acted as if they were leaders of society, whereas a lot of them turned out to be practically wringing out bathing suits in Palm Beach. Speaking of which I will remark that the hardened cocktail party-goer, female, makes Ivan the Terrible look like Winnie-the-Pooh, she is so hard and tough. She always screams louder and longer than anyone in the room, thinking it makes her distinguished (and she is, the distinguished eardrum-splitting champion of the Atlantic Seaboard). She runs up and makes a production out of greeting you, though she's seen you just the other day, with yowls of "I waved to you in the Colony the other day. Did you see me? Did you go to the Snirts' party? Are you invited to the Moos' dinner?" While you, poor slob, can't think of anything to say. But she goes right on. "Isn't this hat divine? Mr. John made it. He makes all my hats, you know." She doesn't want an answer, she loves the scream of her own voice and as soon as someone new comes in she'll pounce on them and set you free.

I also noticed that at every cocktail party there's the girl who sits in a chair in the corner, all by herself, unspoken to, not talking to anyone. She just sits there, perfectly content, until she leaves. Without having said a word.

That's one thing that I wished would have happened

in my early cocktail party going days. I mean I wished that a gong would go off to signify the end of a party. It's hard to tell when to leave a party. I only got caught once. That was at a gay cocktail party where there were movie stars and all sorts of well-known people. I was having a grand time and the party flew by and everyone started to make plans for dinner. They must have assumed that I already had a date; no one asked me to come along. Everyone else was going on to dinner except another girl and me. We were left sitting. What was worse, we had to ride down in the elevator with the others and get a taxi right in front of them. I've never been so mad in all my life. That taught me one thing, though: If you're at a party and people are making dinner plans, if they haven't asked you, jump up right away and pretend you've remembered a dinner engagement and have to hurry because you're already late.

Some of the characters who go to those parties are just amazing. It's hard to believe, but some of the girls that go to them are dirty—really grimy. There they are, in chic dresses, their make-up six feet deep, with another six feet of dirt under their fingernails. There was one particularly, beautiful as a madonna, who would come in, stockingless, coat on coat of powder on her face, her dress covered with spots, and sit on the sofa and smile continuously. There was a pool on to see who could catch her not smiling; but no one ever caught her. She was filthy dirty and always smiling.

These cocktail parties were different, all right; not cocktails before dinner but adventures, mass intrigues. People met at them, fell in love at them, out of love too, got revenges, insulted people, and generally carried on an important part of their lives at them. I have even known brilliant marriages to result from these piddling little cocktail parties.

One thing that's sure is, that at most of these cocktail parties, there are no cocktails. It's tall drinks, whisky and water, because a highball is easier to make and serve, and the glasses don't get broken or spill as easily. I once wondered whether the "party" part was right, either. A man called me, invited me to a party. I went over and there were four people sitting around a small room.

I was in all the columns, mostly for being engaged (if I'd been engaged as much as they said I had, I'd have been one busy girl). Before long, I knew, as I said, everybody of importance: playboys, diplomats, dukes, potentates, counts, governors, political bigwigs, generals . . . even a Chinese general. It was mad.

One of the first times I was engaged, I was engaged to a South American diplomat. He was wonderful. He was tall, dark, and handsome, was high up in his country's government, and was going back there. I was going to join him and we were going to be married. I had dreams of him being president, and I don't know what all. Well, he had gone and I had arranged for my sailing and was going too. In fact, I had just had my trunks taken away to be shipped to South America. I was coming back to the apartment. On the way up in the elevator, as always, I bought a paper and started to read it. My eye fell on something awful. There had been a revolution and my diplomat's government was overthrown; practically all of them were in jail. He wasn't, only because he hadn't got there yet. I went right down again and rushed to the pier. It took me almost three hours to get my trunks off, but I did it in the end. They were off, the engagement was off, everything was off in fact; and that was the last time I heard of him or from him again.

My next flier in romance was with a steel magnate. Horses broke that up. I mean, he was so fond of horses that I didn't dare bend over with the man for fear he would throw a saddle on my back. I love animals myself, and I put up with it pretty well. Until we visited his ranch. It was then he took me out to show me his prize horse named Happy One. That horse should have been happy; I've never seen such surroundings and luxury, and I don't mean for a horse, I mean for people. I noted that that horse's stable was bigger than Junie's and my apartment, bigger and nicer than our apartment, and something inside of me snapped. I left that magnate with his feed bags and currycombs, which is undoubtedly where he is today, and I'll bet Happy One is just glowing.

Junie was right in there pitching, too. At that time she decided she was madly in love with a man who was spending the summer at Easthampton. She also decided that she must go out there for a big party he was giving, and she arranged for me to go out with his brother. I wasn't mad for the brother, but he was all right, so I agreed. We hired a car and chauffeur to drive out there, just for the evening of the party. It was a perfectly brilliant party, and I must say we had quite a bit of champagne. We decided we'd better stay the night and managed to get to our room in the hotel where we were staying, about five in the morning. Not until we woke up the following afternoon did we find out that our room was on a level with the street. We hadn't bothered to draw the shade and there was quite a crowd outside the window. They look pleased and interested. In spite of this mishap, we stayed there three days and had a wonderful time. The only thing that worried us a little was the chauffeur. We asked him if he minded being away so much longer than he expected. He said no; once a man had hired him to drive around Central Park and he wound up in Canada as part of a hunting trip. His wife understood. So we enjoyed ourselves without anything to worry us at all.

Junie was always falling in love. Each time she fell in love just as madly as before, though the romances didn't seem to leave any traces after they faded. The one with the Easthampton fellow didn't turn out so well, though I must say that Junie had the last word. Now Junie, when she loved a man, if she had twenty dollars in her pocket would spend forty on him. This time she went out and got him a beautiful leather writing case, all initialed. It was gorgeous and he loved it, and thanked her for it over and over. The next night, however, he called Junie and broke their date. He was back in town, so Junie took it upon herself to go over to his place. She rang the bell, he opened the door, and there was another girl sitting with him in the living room. Junie just marched herself into the bedroom, took the writing case, marched back to the living room, and threw it into the fireplace. A fire was burning; it was a cold night. It was a cold night for that man. Junie walked out and never spoke to him again.

Winter was coming and it was bringing us problems. Since we were being so elegant we felt the need of furs. We took an inventory and found that we weren't what you would call lousy with mink. Junie had an ermine cape and I had a three-quarter length beaver coat, which Junie could use as a full length one. We decided if Junie went to lunch she could wear my beaver and if I were being especially gala at night I could wear her ermine. Otherwise the beaver would do for me in the evenings too.

"But what if we both go to lunch, Doris?" Junie asked.

"That's a very good question, pigeon," I said, "but it looks like it will never be." And for one year we never had lunch together.

Around then I went on an Indian prince kick for a while. There was one I liked especially. He was cute; he had emerald buttons on his coat. He had just one fault, and that was a complete disregard for our social conventions. He would do the most outrageous things any time, any place. I would get mad at him and chase him around with a tennis racquet. He was small and I really frightened him, so he hired a huge Punjabi servant to be his bodyguard. When I'd start for him he'd shout, "Protect me, protect me, or Miss Lilly will do me hurt." When he went back to India he promised to send me all sorts of things. What I got was a postcard, showing the hotel he was staying at, with an arrow drawn in pointing to a window. A note on the back read: "This is my room." He told me any time I dropped around to India he would show me a glorious time. So any old time I happen to be running around the corner to China, I'll just drop in on India and take him up on his promise.

There were other Indian princes, but they weren't as cute, they didn't have emerald buttons on their coats, and gradually I got tired of the whole thing.

I met a sultan once, and thought I might take to sultans for a bit. When this one said good-by at the party, he told me that if I ever came to his country he would be glad to own me. "Strange mistake in English," I said to a friend when the sultan had left. "Mistake nothing," he said. "The sultan said own and he meant own. He meant you to be in his harem along with his other forty wives." I decided to draw the line at princes and forgot sultans entirely.

Naturally since I went to all these parties I was going on to the night clubs too; mostly El Morocco, the Stork Club, and Twenty One. (In fact if a man asked me to go to a little place for dinner, or to the movies, I'd be insulted; I would wonder, Who does he think he is? He must be out of his Chinese mind.) Too much has been said and written about these night clubs for me to add anything, but I will add something to the pile of information about café society.

The people in café society build their lives around going to night clubs, knowing headwaiters and having headwaiters know them, recognizing the latest show tunes, doing the rhumba without being too obvious but getting the point across just the same. They pride themselves on having inside information on all the doings around town from romances to murders. They're always saying, "Just got back from the Coast," or "I'm off to the south of France for a while." They rarely have homes in the country. Instead they go to California and put in two months at Mocambo. Though there's a great difference between society and café society, the people in café society aren't aware that there's anything better in the world. All they want to do is be seen and see other people like themselves. And they'll do a lot to gain this objective. Some people in café society have press agents, though they would never admit to it, and cry with fake horror when they see something about themselves in the newspapers: "How did *that* get in?"

There are some bad cases of publicity-itis. For instance there was a rather wealthy shoeman who'd always be in Twenty One by himself, waiting around. I'll call him Joe. One day I said hello to him, thinking he looked lonely. "Have you seen John?" he asked me, naming a rich and well-known playboy. "I'm supposed to have lunch with him." "No, I haven't," I told him. I had my lunch, walked around the corner and happened to run into John. "Did you find your friend?" I asked him. "What friend?" he asked. "Joe So-and-so," I said and added, "you were supposed to have lunch with him." "I never laid eyes on him in my life," cried John in amazement.

Yet the shoeman is happy with his dream lunches and

essentially he's not so different from someone like John as someone like John might suppose. Then there was another man who used to come into El Morocco night after night, carrying lots of packages. He'd sit and eat dinner by himself, night after night, alone, but I guess he saw himself as part of the gay throng.

It's all the same really. Some night clubs write down the names of important people in a book as they come in, and leave the book at the door. There are those in café society who won't go into a place unless the book shows that there's a crown prince or so there.

Some people in café society have money, some don't. They all spend it where it shows and think nothing of dropping a couple of hundred dollars at a night club in one evening. But if you were sick and didn't have a thing to eat I wonder how many of them would help you out. Even when they're well I know a lot of girls who would rather have the money than the big evening.

It's fun though, and I enjoyed it for a while, and a lot of amusing things happened to me. I was once in one of those night clubs with a well-known Hollywood star. As we were going out all the cameramen were there taking pictures. Though it was a snowy, blustery evening, I wanted to look as well as I could. I remembered that one is not supposed to look down at the stairs but is supposed to look beforehand and make a mental note of the number of steps. I looked and made a mental note of four steps and walked down, my head held high, looking very haughty. My count was right, but I hadn't seen that the last step was covered with ice. I put my foot on it, slipped, sailed over the sidewalk and lit right in the gutter. Apparently the star had a sense of humor. He thought it was cute, just laughed and laughed.

I enjoyed night clubbing with playboys too. They're attractive, good dancers, well dressed, generally have nice cars. They set a girl off. You don't see much of them when you're out on a date; they're too busy running around a night club or a party getting themselves dates for the next two weeks. It's a little hazardous besides. If you're out in a night club with a man who goes around a lot you never know when a jealous woman is going to throw a glass of champagne in your face or sneak up behind you and clonk you with a bottle of Scotch.

I didn't get wounded but it was about this time when I got charm and had a change of heart. I began to feel funny when the man who was going around with me and who claimed to love me took me out to El Morocco every night for three weeks. I put up with it as long as that and then I said to myself, "This isn't love. How shallow these people who own the place must think we are, coming in here night after night." I was ashamed, *ashamed*.

So I started to stay home more. I gave up a lot of the night clubbers and it was worth it. I had met a man who was most attractive and an intellectual too, and I told myself that he was the one. I had something to learn, though. I was overconfident. An ugly girl came along and took that man away from me like she was driving a Bugatti and I was standing still. She was downright ugly, but she had charm. There was no denying it, and I didn't have charm at that time.

I made up my mind then and there that I would get charm. Instead of reading gossip columns and yakking, I kept quiet, watched, listened, and found out a lot. It's an art not to bore a man, especially one with whom you may not have any friends or interests in common, but charm will do it and charm can be learned. So I learned it.

And also, I saw two other things. One was that I was tired of going out all the time. I wasn't real café society, because with them, it's endless. They never have enough of seeing and being seen. It's not for one year, for three, or for ten, it's forever. "Doris," I said to myself, "this is where you step off."

The other thing I saw was that men of all kinds have much more respect and admiration for a successful career girl than for one whose whole attitude is glamour and on the town.

I got myself a job.

This sounds terribly serious; really, the job I got was pretty funny. While I was asking around to see what was available, I heard from a friend who had been told by another friend who knew someone who knew that there was a job open on a fashion magazine. The name of the fashion magazine was *Beau Monde,* and the job was being accessory editor. I hadn't been any kind of an editor before, but I had been wearing stockings, scarves, jewelry, gloves, and carrying handbags most of my life, so I thought I would give it a try. Besides, I had always had compliments on the way I dressed.

People who were pretty chic themselves thought I had real good taste.

I phoned *Beau Monde* for an appointment, and got one. In spite of my good taste, I spent the whole day getting my hair done and buying a new outfit. From what I had seen of it, the best was only half good enough for *Beau Monde*.

The next afternoon I showed up at the office of *Beau Monde*. By this time, I had worked myself up to the point where I was kind of wild eyed, and my hands were damp inside my suède gloves. The reception room of the magazine didn't make me any more relaxed. It was awfully pink, and there was only one big desk in it. At the desk was sitting an old lady with a lot of white hair piled up on her head. She was whispering into the telephone like she was some kind of priestess, and couldn't talk any louder because it would have been sacrilegious. She told me to wait, that the beauty editor would see me in a few minutes. Half an hour later the beauty editor came in. To pass the time, I had been looking through some copies of *Beau Monde*. My outfit, which had looked so good to me not more than an hour before, now seemed to me like a bundle of rags. My suède gloves were practically soaked through.

But the beauty editor couldn't have been nicer. She said her name was Miss Prist, and how was I? I didn't tell her how I was. Instead I lied, and told her I was feeling great. Then we talked about where we had come from, people we both knew, how hard it was to find apartments, and the high price of food. At first I kept trying to lead the conversation around to things like, would I get the job? Then I gave up and let her wander on, while I sneaked glances at her hair, her make-up, and her clothes. They were all terrific, and I could see that she sure knew how to use beauty products—in a subtle way, of course.

In the middle of telling how the landlord had made her sign a twelve-year lease on the place she was living in, Miss Prist looked at her watch, and said we had to go on up now. Mrs. Welter would be waiting for us.

The elevator took us up five floors, and Miss Prist took me to the waiting room of Mrs. Welter's office. I could see right away that Mrs. Welter was a big wheel on *Beau Monde*. And she really was earning her salary. Her office was a businesslike gray; three telephones were ringing their heads off. She had to have two secretaries just to keep the traffic moving. The only difference between Mrs. Welter's office and Fifth Avenue was that in her office the traffic was all on foot. Once I thought I saw a taxi wheel in, but I guess that was just my nerves.

At the end of fifteen minutes, Mrs. Welter called for Miss Prist. Miss Prist, leading me by the hand, took me up to Mrs. Welter's desk, all the while telling her about me. I felt like Mrs. Welter was a school principal, and I was a kid in line to skip a grade.

Mrs. Welter's approach was the opposite of Miss Prist's. She threw a pile of photographs on the floor (the entire carpet was littered with pictures and heaps of paper), gave me a smile that would have blinded the girl in a cigarette ad, and asked me twenty-five practical questions in the space of eight minutes. I answered her as best I could, though I couldn't match her for speed. While we were going through our tobacco-auction routine, I couldn't help comparing her with the beauty editor.

I could see right off that Mrs. Welter was above the minor worries of being slick and well groomed. In fact it was hard to tell if she fixed her hair with a comb or a Waring mixer. But I could tell her simple little hat had set her back a young fortune, even if she treated it as casually as she did. It never stayed in one place. When we started questions-and-answers, she was wearing it sideways, sitting on her eyebrows. At the end of the interview she had turned it around, so it was backside to, hanging over her right ear.

While I was still telling her about what I had been doing in New York, and how my grandmother always told me I had lovely taste, a whole new gang of people rushed in the door. Mrs. Welter gave me that smile again. I guessed the interview was over. Pushing my way out the door, I saw her shove her hat over her left ear, which gave the other one clearance for the phone; she said something to a pale thin man, threw him a bundle of papers. He caught them (pretty neat catch, I thought), and ran down the corridor with them, shouting, "It's mauve, it's mauve, Miss M., I told you it was!" I never did find out what Miss M. thought of mauve, because we had turned a couple of corners, and were in Miss Thornless's office.

I didn't need to be told that Miss Thornless was the biggest wheel of all on *Beau Monde*. Her secretaries were so elegant they could hardly lift up their heads.

With every sentence, they sounded as if they were going to call me an upstart, only they were too exhausted to bother that day.

Miss Thornless's office was size huge, and looked more like someone's snappy drawing room than an office. Miss Thornless had blue hair, and she was perfect. That's all I can say... *perfect*. Her hair and her suit, her rings, her fingernails... everything was perfect. She was looking at the ceiling, as if she was wondering if it would fall down or not. I guess she decided finally it would hold for a while longer anyway. She looked at me, and told me what I would have to do. I didn't hear half what she said, because she was whispering. First I thought she had a cold or something, but I found out later she always whispered. I guess the struggle to make women wear the right things just wore her out. She sounded twice as tired as her secretaries.

Then, turning her face to one side as if she was speaking of something ugly, she mentioned money. She told me that, beautiful a magazine as *Beau Monde* was, it had a budget. The nasty publisher insisted on it. Did I by any chance have a private income? I told her I was sorry I didn't; thinking, why would I want a job if I had a private income? She explained that because of that dirty old budget *Beau Monde* could only pay me what she called a rather moderate salary. The salary she named was moderate all right, but I was so dazzled and impressed that it sounded grand to me. Miss Thornless went back to looking at the ceiling, Miss Prist and I tiptoed out, and I was an accessory editor on *Beau Monde* magazine.

I tried. I worked like a dog for *Beau Monde*. I learned so much my first month there I thought my head would fly open. But it was no use. I couldn't fit into that chi-chi world. All those women running around cackling, "Dahling, it's a *great* new thing in kid shoes," or "I've just lost my reason over that pumpkin-colored shirt," or "Sweetie, that new shade of lipstick makes me a little bit sick." It made me more than a little bit sick myself. I couldn't bring myself to care that much about clothes. After all, you put them on your back, and that's nice, but it isn't printing the Gutenberg Bible when you come right down to it. Also, all the women there were fighting like crazy. We would go to meetings which were supposed to help make the magazine run more smoothly. Those meetings nearly always wound up when one editor called another editor a "fat, old *thing*," and the other editor rushed out crying like mad. I don't believe in fighting. All my life I had gotten along without it, and I wasn't going to break the habit even for *Beau Monde*.

Then there was the salary. I was surprised that people weren't dying like flies in their offices from starvation. They must have all had private incomes, all right. I was getting by, but the fact was that I was earning the same salary as our maid, and she didn't have to get to work till one in the afternoon while I had to be in the office at nine sharp. It made me aggravated. And prices were going up all the time.

So I bootlegged. I smuggled a second job into my main one on *Beau Monde*. With the help of friends, I started doing publicity. I promoted actors and band leaders and cosmetics and soft drinks. In fact, before I left, I was running a regular publicity bureau right from my *Beau Monde* office, making my calls on their phone, and sending out releases on their stationery. What got them finally was that I was doing publicity for too many of the "low" Broadway types they despised so much.

I wasn't surprised when I was called into Miss Thornless's office and told *Beau Monde* would have to let me go. The "lowness" of my extra work was what was making her unhappy. "How could you, my dear?" she wanted to know. "Unwholesome's Cold Cream, Grit Nail Polish... products we have never, never favored. And Tony Rejecto—a *band* leader of sorts, I believe. Not to mention crooners and persons of that nature. No, I'm afraid it can't go on. I'm so sorry, we had such hopes for you."

They may have had hopes for me, but after six months with *Beau Monde* I was down to the point where all I could hope for was the price of a jar of peanut butter. Still, we said good-by on good terms. They went their way, and I went mine. My way was publicity, regular publicity I didn't have to hide, which was my job from then on.

Life with Junie was still mad and hectic. She'd decided to take a job too, with a chorus. I was horrified. "But, Doris," she said, "I don't have your brains. I can dance, though, and I want to go down South later this winter. The chorus is going South." I pointed out that it would be a lot easier to get a sun lamp, but she would hear none of it. Which was Junie all over. Impulsive. And she was kindhearted—so much so that it was a trial sometimes. She'd be out of the place half an hour and the packages would start coming in. She'd go in somewhere and buy a two-hundred-dollar dress because she felt sorry for the salesgirl. The dress would usually go to the cleaner's once and come back fit for a Lilliputian. She used to make great friends out of maids, have dinner with them, visit their families. I'd come back from a trip and say to the maid, "Would you take these clothes to the cleaner's for me?" and the maid would immediately get sore, say, "Who does she think she is, talking to me like that?" and quit.

Then there was the business of the fur coat. Junie had twenty-five hundred dollars with which to get a fur coat. After she had carried it around for two weeks pinned to a change purse and nearly driven me out of my mind, I persuaded her to come with me to a wholesale furrier's. First he showed her a lovely mink. No, she didn't think that was very nice. After all, everyone had mink. Then he brought out a Russian fitch. It looked liked a tent with a hole in the middle, not to mention the color or the practicality of it. "Junie, wouldn't the mink be better?" I hinted. She loved the fitch, nothing would do but the fitch. She got the fitch. In six months that fitch turned bright yellow and the black tips all fell out. In a year it looked like a terry bath mat.

But I didn't worry about Junie. If she went to Cuba she'd fall in love with the owner of the biggest sugar plantation there; if she went to Florida, she would adore the man with the most orange groves; if she went to Boston, it was the man who owned the bean factories. I remember, in our old apartment, we had no central heating and I once got so desperate for warmth that I tore the shelves out of the kitchen and burned them in the fireplace. She told me I oughtn't to do it. When I asked her, "Pigeon, what *will* we do?" she got hold of some stove king and we had our pick of a shipment of stoves right away.

Junie was a big help to me at this stage. She was domestic and knew how to cook, and she taught me. I wanted to learn, because by this time I was going around with the conservative type of millionaire. I knew so many kinds of millionaires that I was getting choosy, and I picked on the conservative kind because he was substantial and a nice change from the café society type.

The conservative millionaire doesn't like to go to night clubs, he'd much rather stay in. He has complete contempt for headwaiters and all the red tape of that sort, and when he goes out is liable to go to a private party. (When he does put in an appearance at a night club, he gets the best table in the house, without tipping a soul.) The conservative millionaire is social, has had money for several generations, and is mainly interested in two things: making more money (which includes saving what he's got in small ways), and his social obligations.

This kind of man wouldn't think of traveling to business in a taxi. No, he puts on his Homburg and rides the subway, explaining with great joy that it saves him eight and a half minutes each way, each day. Not to mention a dollar or so. He loves to buy a yacht, use it for a year, then sell it for more than he paid for it originally. He's crafty, and loves to get something, anything, from a house to a cocktail shaker, cheaper than the market price, and he'll brag about it endlessly to his friends.

He works, and really works, like a dog. Just as if he had to. He loves to tell you that he went down to the Street (Wall, that is) this morning, and that it looked terrible, terrible. He'd rather have it look terrible than have it look good, because he knows *why* it looks terrible, and he isn't going to tell you... it's a big, mad secret.

All this concern is probably why the guy has this money to begin with, but even so, it gets to be a little funny. I had a wonderful story told to me about one of these men: A dowager was walking along in Newport, when she came upon one of the local young men kneeling on the ground, groaning loudly, and eating grass. "What on earth are you eating grass for?" she asked. "I haven't any money. I'm hungry and I haven't had anything to eat for three days. That's why I'm eating grass," he answered. "For Heaven's sake, young man," she cried, "why don't you dip into your principal?" This may be a joke, but there's a lot of truth in it.

As for the social obligations, those too are very dear to his heart, though you might not think so at first. Everything is a bore, to hear him talk, he doesn't really want to go anywhere at all. "I *have* to go to the Ramseys' on Saturday. It's so ghastly, and it's *so* boring, but

I *have* to go." Or it's, "Oh, my God, it's the Fish-head Ball on Tuesday. I thought I'd die last year it was so awful, I guess I'll have to suffer through it though." If you ask him why, why does he have to do all these things, he'll say, "Oh, they asked me three weeks ago, and I just have to put in an appearance. You know how these things are." But you don't know how these things are. The truth is, if he didn't get an invitation to the Ramseys' or the Fish-head Ball, he'd go out after a while and cut off his head. He won't go willingly; he *has* to go. Going gladly or not being invited would be the death of him.

He never has any cash on him and is always stopping off at one of his clubs to cash a check. His suits, though attractive, look vaguely as if he had put one on, been dunked in the East River a couple of times, and just kept it on after it had dried out.

There are a lot of nice things about him, too. He's kind, considerate in a lot of ways, much more sincere than the café society stars, more fun to be with, because he is liable to like to talk. He often talks quite intelligently, and has a fairly sensible attitude toward life. He won't give you expensive presents. You're liable to spend more money on him, making home-cooked dinners and homemade drinks, than he will on you. But he likes a girl with interests of her own, particularly a girl with a successful career, has a lot of respect for her, and certainly would make a very good husband.

As I was bending over the stove fixing dinners, I would think, "I've come a long way in search of millionaires, all the way from Santa Monica to New York, and

I know a dozen different kinds of millionaires, but this is the strangest thing of all. When you were home in California you used to stay in and help around the house, and all you wanted to do was to get out and see the glittering world. Now you've seen the glittering world, and all they want you to do is stay home and cook. There's one thing that life is, to coin a phrase, Doris, and that's strange, mighty strange."

CHAPTER 4

FOREIGN LANDS: VERMONT, CHICAGO, MEXICO

THE STRANGENESS HAD ONLY BEGUN. I cooked a series of meals for a series of homebody millionaires until I could cook a lot of things: soufflés, roasts, all sorts of dishes. The last of this type of man was real distinguished, though he actually wasn't a true millionaire. But he lived like one, and he was from an old and distinguished European family. In fact, he was the Prince of a small European country to which I'll give the mythical name of Nordland. Of course, Nordland had been overrun in the war, and hadn't been a monarchy for some time before that. Ludwig was pretty impressive, a pretender to a throne, in spite of his drawbacks. Smallness was one of them; looking like a poodle was another.

Don't misunderstand me, I'm fond of poodles, just not when they're men, if you see what I mean. Lots of people saw what I meant about Ludwig. He had black clustering hair like a poodle, round, gluey eyes like a poodle, and his whole face came to the fore in the middle. He had a snout, I should say nose, like a poodle. He was sweet, however, and had lots of charm. (I know what you're thinking, but it wasn't much like a poodle's sweetness and charm.) Besides, he was filled with gallantry and stories about Europe and the glorious past. And he was mad for me, just mad for me.

Junie didn't think too much of him. She thought he was sweet and all, she just took an irreverent attitude. She'd say: "What are you getting dressed up for, Doris? Is the Poodle Prince coming tonight? If he is, why cook dinner? Just open a can of Red Heart."

I thought this was going too far, and I told her so. I said, "Junie, instead of making remarks about dog food, why don't you do what I do? Study the Nordlandian language the way I am, and listen to the records of that lovely old European music I bought. Then maybe you'll learn something."

I was really studying the language and listening to the music. I was also learning about the genealogies of noble European families, especially royal families. It's something I do with every beau. With the princes, it was Indian customs; with the steel magnate, it was bloodlines of horses. I started to learn Spanish for the diplomat, and the conservative millionaires had taught me a lot about corporation laws and high finance in general.

Ludwig didn't like to go out, because of the publicity. He said he hated publicity, though every time we did go out, or even when we didn't, our names would be in dozens of columns, sometimes with pictures. To tell the truth, I suspected him of secretly having a press agent. Anyway, this fear he expressed of publicity caused us to go only to tiny, badly lit bistros with wine-smeared tablecloths, where the food was often as greasy as the atmosphere. This I didn't care for in the least, and I used to argue with him about it. "Ludwig," I would say, "since our pictures are always in the papers anyway, why can't we go to El Morocco, or the Stork, or Twenty One? What difference would it make if the columnists said we were seen in Morocco instead of La Gravy Stain Café? Except that it would be nicer?" But he would have none of it, and the upshot was we sat around Junie's and my place most of the time, listening to music and drinking Nordlandian-type liquors (very strong). I had fun on the whole, though. Ludwig was easy to get along with, and it *was* impressive. The impressiveness is what really got me. I will never forget the time the tie salesman put a crimp in the glamour of it all.

This salesman came around to the back door, selling ties. I went to talk to him, and just my luck, he had recently come over from Nordland. He kept on talking about Nordland, about how he loved it, and what a fine country it was. He was a refugee, and the ties were nice, so I bought some. Then, thinking I would give him a thrill, I said to him confidentially, "Who do you think is going to wear these ties?" "Who?" he said, excited. "Prince Ludwig," I whispered. "Who?" he asked, blank as an egg. "Prince Ludwig," I said, louder. "Oh," he said, looking brighter, "a prince. Yes, Russians like these ties." "Look," I said (by this time I was shouting), "look, Prince Ludwig of Nordland, you know, your country, the man who would be on the throne after his mother, the queen, died." The tie salesman just looked at me with moist eyes. "There isn't any throne any more," he said after a minute, "so what's the fuss about?" I had to admit he had something there; and it even made me feel low for a while. But I recovered.

This went on for a while. Then Ludwig asked me to marry him. I thought it over. It was a hard decision. I wasn't in love with him (I told him I wasn't, and he was still willing), and close up the royalty business was a little awkward. I couldn't seem myself walking into Toots Shor's as Princess Doris of Nordland. My friends would think it was a little silly, and I thought it was pretty silly too. On the other hand, Ludwig was steady, quiet, and a nice person, and I felt that year it was time for me to get married. So I said, "Yes." And once I had made up my mind, I threw myself into the whole thing with gusto.

Ludwig was often in Philadelphia on business; on week ends I would go down to visit him and stay with his cousin who lived there. She was an ardent Nordlandian too, very active in Relief for Nordland, head of its Philadelphia branch. I was very much affected by her stories of the sufferings of Nordland, and offered to work for the cause in New York. She could see I meant business, and she made me head of the New York branch. I worked like a dog for Nordland Relief. I got blankets, household things, hats, coats, dresses, shoes, sweaters, I don't know what all from my friends, besides lots of things from various owners of department stores I knew. I sent tons and tons of the stuff to Nordland, three huge shipments, and had collected a fourth that filled an entire room in the apartment, floor to ceiling, when I was interrupted in my work.

Ludwig appeared one evening, in a state. He told me he was going up to Vermont to see his mother the next day, and would I join him a few days later. She wanted to meet me. I said sure I would and that I'd like to meet her too. It was all settled and Ludwig left happy, though he seemed a little put out that I hadn't been more impressed by an invitation to meet a queen. The fact was, nothing surprised me any more.

I packed my warm clothes, booked a reservation, and three days later, in the late afternoon, I was in the north of Vermont. It was a pretty trip; the place was snowy and nice the way I had imagined it would be. Ludwig was there to meet me at the station, but without a conveyance of any kind. He'd sent his car back, and I don't know how he thought we were going to get to his mother's place. So I hired a car and chauffeur finally, and we drove out to the Queen's house.

It was fairly modest; the grounds were very large and well kept. I didn't think it looked forbidding. I told the chauffeur to wait, as I didn't know whether I was to stay here, or in the town, and Ludwig couldn't tell me what the plans were. The minute I got inside, three servants hustled me into the drawing room, without giving me a chance to take off my coat. As they bore me away, I looked around for Ludwig. He had vanished—was nowhere in sight.

The Queen was standing in the drawing room, waiting for me. I didn't know whether to curtsy or bow or what, so I bent, sort of, and said, "How do you do?" She said, "Good afternoon, Miss Lilly," and we both sat down. For the first time I got a good look at her. She was elderly, white haired, small, dressed in old-fashioned clothes, and very haughty, which was helped by her nose. She had the kind of nose which if she looked up would make her appear to be looking down. If her son looked like a poodle, it struck me his mother sure resembled a pelican, and an awful pun about bird dog floated through my head. Without a pause, she said, "Before we go any farther" (How far can you go? I thought to myself), "there is one request I have of you. Will you please give me the name of your solicitors in New York or California or wherever they may be? I would like to speak to them about your financial condition. You see, none of my sons has ever married against my wishes; I do not object to you but I want to be sure that you can support yourself and contribute something to help maintain the family in general as well. With us, the family is most important."

I was stunned for a minute. I thought, should I be offended? Then I thought, "Why? What do I want to get offended about? After all, I need him like I need a second head, and his family like I need a third one."

So I said to her, "Madame, you do not have to call my solicitors. I can tell you about my finances, and I can say what I have to say to you in a few minutes. About my finances: I suppose I have in the neighborhood, oh, let's put is conservatively, of around five million dollars... in real estate, investments of different kinds, annuities, and an irrevocable trust. I have a house in California, a house in Mexico and one in Bermuda, a few race horses, and I guess that's about the sum total of things."

Of course none of this was true, but it was too good a chance to resist, and besides I wasn't going to let that old Queen insult me and get away with it. I was going to add that rumor had it my house in California was responsible for the servant shortage on the entire West Coast; but I thought that might be going a little too far. I went on: "*And* I might add that my family has been opposed to my intended marriage to your son from the time they heard about it. I came here primarily to see you and tell you that I can't marry him. I thought it was the courteous thing to do. I'm definitely not going to marry Ludwig."

She sat there without saying a word, but I could see that she wanted to bite her tongue off. I got up and said, "Thank you for your generosity and kindness, and I feel sure that your son will have no trouble marrying a very wealthy woman."

I walked out of the room and passed Ludwig, who was standing in the hall like he was a marble monument, and went right outside to the car which was still waiting. (It hadn't had long to wait, God knows.) Ludwig ran out of the house, through the snow, shouting, "Dorees, Dorees, darleeng, wait, wait, don't go this way." He climbed in the car, and we drove back to the airport. I told him that nothing could change my mind, that I was taking the next plane back to New York, and I wasn't going to marry him, or even see him again if I could help it. At the airport I found out that I had to wait three hours for the next plane back to the city. For three hours we sat in the airport, and for three hours Ludwig didn't stop pleading with me, telling me he loved me and wanted me to marry him, and that his mother didn't mean anything by it, she was just that way. I told him, "Ludwig, maybe that's the way it is, but I'm the way *I* am—I'm not going to marry you and that's that."

The plane came and I took it, leaving Ludwig to go back to the house and have a swell talk with mama. When I got back to the apartment, the first thing that caught my eye was that roomful of clothes and stuff that was going to Nordland. Somehow that made me madder than anything had. The next day I called up another organization and every single article in the room got sent to the British. I hope they enjoyed the things.

I got over my first anger, and I saw Ludwig around town a number of times after that. He finally got married. She didn't have money, but when her mother-in-law walks into a room, that girl's knees buckle, just buckle, so I guess everyone is happy all the way around.

Junie was awfully nice about the whole episode, and never mentioned dog food to me once. She could see I was moping around, and night after night she'd try to cheer me up before I went out. I still felt blue because I was plain disillusioned; and on top of everything,

Junie was going South with the chorus soon, which made me feel lonely in advance. But one afternoon, when I was feeling worse than usual (my best perfume broke to add to all my other troubles), she told me, "Listen, why stay in the city while I am down South? Travel while I am gone; get some sunshine and new faces and away from it all."

I saw in a flash she was right. I had to get out of town, stop thinking of all the angles to millionaires for a while, and just relax. When she left, I left too. We closed the apartment; Junie headed South, and I headed West. I figured I would go out to California, see my parents, and then take off for Mexico, and visit friends I had there.

Everything went smoothly as far as Chicago. I'd only been able to get a ticket as far as Chicago, so I got off the train there, planning to get a ticket out to California. The ticket agent practically told me I was nothing better than a wild dreamer. He pointed out that Chicago was jammed and packed, and he didn't know when I'd be able to get out.

I realized I needed time to think, so I got a room in Chicago's nicest hotel, and thought. Junie had given me the name of a friend of hers who lived in Chicago, just in case I needed anything while I was there. She told me he was the perfect person to straighten out difficulties. His name was Petey, and I gave him an immediate call. His voice was nice, he was very polite and he thought he could arrange something all right... but he couldn't possibly get anything till the next day, and would I have dinner with him that night? I couldn't see sitting around a perfectly strange town, counting the pedestrians that were knocked flat by the famous wind; I told him, fine.

And it was, during dinner. He was nice looking in a certain kind of way, with a squarish head, curly blond hair, and pale skin. He was the kind of guy who looked as if his only exercise was walking back and forth at the racetrack, from the grandstand to the betting windows, carrying heavy armfuls of cash. And he did his best to help that impression along. He was pretty sinister by nature, probably, but he put it on some too. I guess he thought it was awfully smart. He never talked, he whispered; even "Two more Martinis" was breathed out, barely loud enough for the waiter to hear. At first I thought people were listening to us or something, and was kind of scared; then I saw that they weren't; and relaxed.

After dinner (which was in the Pump Room and a wonderful dinner), he asked me if I minded driving out with him to pick up some business papers before we went on. I told him, of course not, and off we drove.

We drove for what seemed to me a long way, and I got scared again, not only because of him, but because of the city itself. There's something queer about Chicago at least to me. What I mean is, other places have something to hold them together; in California, it's the trees, in New York, it's skyscrapers; in Chicago, there isn't anything. Lots of parts of Chicago are pretty and all, but each part is so different; it reminded me of movie sets all strung together, without any connection with each other. Anyway, we drove along, and finally, by the time we got to Petey's office on the outskirts of town, my teeth were chattering so hard I couldn't say a word.

The building we stopped at didn't help any. It was old and ratty, and darker than the inside of a derby hat when it is on someone's head. Petey led the way up a pair of rickety stairs and unlocked a moldy old door. When he turned on the lights the room looked pretty cheerful, in contrast to the rest of the building. It was painted, and had some desks, a few chairs, but the other furniture consisted of telephones, dozens of telephones, plus a few loudspeakers, and odd-looking radios. It dawned on me after an instant: "A bookie," I thought, "a bookie or maybe a numbers racket," and I almost bolted down the stairs. This I didn't do: instead, I got hold of myself and started to think that if he was so awful and illegal as all that, he wouldn't have brought me to the place. And even if he was bookmaker on the side, I thought, it couldn't be so terribly illegal in Chicago if he let a perfect stranger like myself see what he was up to. So I preserved my calm, didn't act impressed, and in a few minutes we left. He asked me if I'd like to go to a small club or a big place where we could see some local characters. I voted for the characters. Ludwig had temporarily ruined my taste for *intime* spots.

The place we wound up in was something like the West Side night clubs of New York, with some big differences. It was even bigger, it had more chrome, more mirrors; it was darker, for some good reason. Nothing I'd seen in New York held a dim candle to the local characters. Fierce, fierce wasn't the word for it. I can only say that most of them would have looked more at home on four feet than on the two apiece they were featuring that evening. As my eyes got used to the light, or the lack of it, I noticed most of the men's pockets were bulging, and my conclusion was that everyone in the place had two or three machine guns stowed away for handy reference. The more I think about it, the more I think I was so right.

Petey and I sat down, we talked and drank champagne, and I was just beginning to enjoy myself when several hoarse voices shouted, "Hiya Petey." I looked up, and standing a few yards away were the toughest, most unshaven, worst looking pair of hoodlums in the room. Petey obviously didn't want to have much to do with them, and tried to get away with waving, shouting "Hello," and leaving it at that. But no, they jostled their way over to the table, and stood there until Petey made the introductions. "Hi," they said to me. One of them turned to Petey. "Say kid, that's a good lookin' tomato youse has got wit youse. Didya import her or what?" When I saw that this was going to be the tone, I tried to smile, and act natural for Petey's sake.

Too natural, because they got encouraged and the other one said to me, "Like to buy youse a drink." These types looked as if when you said "Hello" to them, they'd be stuck for an answer. I guess "Like to buy youse a drink" really meant something to them, conversationally and socially. I didn't realize how much. I said politely, "No, thank you, you're very nice, but we have lots here, thank you." Wrong move. Right away they got insulted, especially the one who had offered the drink. He got really sore and kept mumbling, "So de broad don't like me. Not good enough for her, hunh, not good enough for her," until my nerves snapped, and I asked them if they wouldn't sit down, and have a glass of champagne with us. That seemed to make things a lot better, and they not only sat down, they waved to four more of their pals to sit down too. So there I sat with six of the worst hoodlums in Chicago, two of whom I later discovered were the most notorious gamblers in the entire city. They had themselves a ball in a sinister sort of way, and didn't seem to care that Petey was looking horribly embarrassed and not saying a word.

By the time we left, which was an hour later, they were my buddies, my friends. Nuttin', they said, was too good for me, and where did I live? I gave them two wrong addresses, one for Chicago and one for New York, and we parted on jovial terms. I got back to the hotel with no further trouble. Petey didn't offer any explanations, and I didn't ask for any. I went to my room and had a good night's sleep—after I'd stopped shaking.

Petey called the next morning to say he'd been able to get the tickets to California. He was working and couldn't get over, so he'd send his chauffeur instead, to deliver the ticket, and take me to the station; he hoped I'd understand. I told him I understood. Though he was nice and attractive, I was just as glad it turned out the way it had, due to his friends and their habits.

I had just finished packing, when the desk clerk phoned to say that Petey's chauffeur was on his way up. I'm glad I was warned: not only was Petey's chauffeur, from all appearances, one of the mobsters, he looked more like a walking general store than a gangster even, he had his arms so full of stuff. "Is youse Miss Lilly?" he asked from behind the pile. "Yes," I answered. "The boss said to give youse dese," and he dumped all the things in my arms. I could hardly believe my eyes: Petey had sent me about three dozen pairs of stockings, four bottles of Scotch, and half a dozen cartons of cigarettes. They were nice presents because of the shortages, but they were only half wrapped, and the chauffeur had walked through the hotel's plush lobby with stockings flying out behind him, Scotch bottles clinking together, and ends of cigarette cartons sticking out of brown paper bags. I could have died of humiliation; all I could think of was to get out of there as fast as I could. The chauffeur, whose name, if you can call it that, turned out to be Sheep, juggled the pile together; he and I and a couple of bellboys made quite a sensation downstairs. All the guests who happened to be in the lobby thought it was better than a show. One man even turned to his wife and said that. "Diana," he said, "this is better than a show."

He should have seen what was waiting outside. Sheep led me to the car, and what a car! It was almost a block long, no exaggeration, black, and bulletproof. It was so bulletproof you could tell it a mile away; I half expected flowers and funeral wreaths to be piled in the back. I ran into it, Sheep slammed the door, and we roared away from the hotel, just about as inconspicuous as an American Legion parade.

All the way to the station Sheep told me stories to keep me amused. They had to do with killings, trials, and things like that. By the time we got there I was so amused the perspiration was standing out on my forehead. We sailed through the station, stockings waving, bottles clashing. Sheep found the head conductor on my train. He said, "Dis tomato is goin' ta California. She's a good friend of Petey's. Take good care of her." With that he handed the man twenty dollars, gave me my ticket, and got all my belongings settled in my drawing room.

The last thing I saw in Chicago was Sheep, waving good-by, his old bullet scars standing out in the bright sunlight, glancing over his shoulder every few seconds. It was certainly a different type experience. I didn't mind it though; in fact, I enjoyed it in a way. I'm sure a lot of nice respectable people live in Chicago; I just didn't meet them, that's all. And when I think about it, you can meet nice respectable people any old time, but Petey and Sheep are special, once-in-a-lifetime characters.

The ride to California was like a dream, it was so pleasant. Sheep had made a definite dent, and I was treated like a queen. It was nice to see my father and mother again; by the time I was ready to go to Mexico, my nerves were in excellent conditon, and Ludwig, and my stay in Chicago seemed very far away.

I had planned to fly to Mexico, but at the last minute I found out that an old friend of the family's was driving down, so I drove with him instead. Geography is not my strong point. I never liked it in school. In this case, I should have looked at a map before blithely waving good-by to Santa Monica civilization, such as it was. From Santa Monica to Tia Juana it was a lovely trip, and not too long; once we were out of Tia Juana, heading for Mexico City, it was too terrible to even think about much. In the first place the distance between the two cities is almost as great as between Chicago and Los Angeles, and in the second place it's absolutely barren country, sagebrush desert, where it was one hundred and two degrees when it was fairly cool, and where we actually had to make our own roads.

The only way we had to guide ourselves was by picking out something on the horizon and driving in that direction. One roasting afternoon we were guiding ourselves by a gasoline pump sticking up against the sky; it made us a little more cheerful as we gasped along, because we were pretty sure that where that gasoline pump was, some kind of oasis must be too. After ghastly hours we got to it, and sure enough, the gasoline pump owner was also the proud proprietor of a desert version bar and grill. The tables were broken and sagging, the chairs too, and the bar was made of sand bags, but not even Twenty One had ever looked half as good to me as that place did. I was just about to plunk myself down at a table and get something to eat and drink, when I noticed a man lying under another table, on his side, with his face turned away from me. The owner spoke some English, so I grabbed him by the arm, and asked him what was the matter with the man, was he drunk or what? He was lying terribly still.

He just shrugged and said he didn't know what the matter was, the man had been lying there since early last night. I think the trail of dust I left getting out of that place must still be hanging in the air. I almost cried when Mexico City came in sight. I promised myself on the spot I would never sneer at any kind of civilization again, no matter what kind it was.

I think Fate was after me on that whole trip, because all I was looking for was rest, peace, and quiet, and all I got was frenzy and outlaws. I had an idea that Mexico City was a slow, country sort of place, where siesta was the high point of the day. Instead, it was one of the gayest, most frenzied towns I've ever seen. Night clubs—it's just jammed with them. It looks as if someone had taken all the night clubs in New York and put them on three streets. When people aren't in the night clubs, they're at parties or giving patries. It's almost as if they are trying to prove to themselves that they are having a high old time. There's something hysterical about it. It's fast, extravagant, and the people there are an odd mixture. Some of them are just usual people of the chic kind; lots of others are running away from something, or can't go back to their own countries. This kind just has fun, fun, fun, all day long and all night, and they never stop for a minute to think, which I guess is the general idea. Someone would give a party; there would be a huge banquet first, and then the host would take over a night club for an evening, and the sky was the limit. If the check came to only a few thousand dollars, the party was considered to be a flop. This was the frenzy I got involved with.

The outlaw was Raquel. He was a real, genuine bandit, who had worked, or shot his way up, until he was a big power in politics and business. He would stomp into a night club, pick out the table he liked best, and demand it. If there happened to be some people sitting at it already, they had to move. Raquel would swagger up to it, knock any glasses or plates that were on it off onto the floor with a sweep of his arm. He would flop into a chair, call for drinks; while they were being brought he'd carefully take his two guns out of their holsters and put them on the table where everyone could see them. Not that anyone had to; they were all terrified of Raquel, and the only revenge they had was not to invite him to the parties, and to snub him generally. Socially, Raquel was a gigantic flop; in fact, it was social death for a girl to be seen anywhere in his vicinity.

One night Raquel came into a night club where I was with a party of other people and took a great fancy to me. Instead of picking out a table of his own, he roared up to ours, had the waiter bring another chair, fixed himself in it, and wouldn't budge. Social flop or no social flop, the friends I was with were too pale with fear to do anything about the situation. He looked pleased as a cat with a bottle of homogenized milk and two roast chickens, but I could not claim to be happy. In the first place, Raquel was no one's dream hero. Even Pancho Villa must have looked a lot better than Raquel did. He was a musty yellow color, like an elderly lemon, he was pock-marked, his handlebar mustache and slicked-back hair was just glistening with oil. Old oil at that, from a whiff I got of it. However, he was trying to be nice, so I did my best to be nice back. Also, there were those two guns right in front of me as a kind of hint to be expansive and pleasant.

After ordering assorted drinks and champagne, Raquel insisted on ordering me dinner. I chose guinea hen; he told the waiter what I wanted in Spanish, and gave his own order. My guinea hen came, looking most attractive. I looked over at Raquel's plate, and turned cold with horror. On his plate was a big, thick steak, which was fine, except that it was raw; cold, stony, dark-purple raw. He salted it, cut it, and ate the entire thing while I watched him, unable to touch my guinea hen. In his bad English, he explained that he always ate raw meat: only at a dinner party, sometimes, to be polite, would he touch it cooked. That was the way things were with Raquel.

Then he asked me to dance. The fact that I had to keep kicking my heels backward into the air to prevent him from mashing my shinbones to a pulp was nothing. You can imagine what someone who has just finished eating a raw steak smells like. It was exactly like dancing with a lion.

Any faint enthusiasm I might have had for glamorous bandits vanished on the spot. Raquel did not feel the same way. He was more enthusiastic over me than ever. He found out my name, and where I was staying, and from that day on, bombarded me with notes, flowers, and huge and expensive presents. At first he demanded that I go out with him; when I didn't answer the notes, threw the flowers out, and returned the presents, he changed his tune a little, and said that he just wanted to see me for a few hours, just be with me and talk to me for a while. It was a trying situation. Everyone was too scared of him to tell him off, and everyone in Mexico City knew about it. I was just chagrined.

Returning the presents made it worse: in Mexico you never know what's going to happen when you send something somewhere, and when I'd go somewhere I'd see a Mexican girl wearing a pin or bracelet I'd supposedly sent back to Raquel, because she was the messenger's wife's third cousin or something. I didn't blame them; I wouldn't want to return a present to Raquel in person. Besides, things were so unfair; these people were giving wild parties and spending money like madmen, while most of the Mexicans were so poor that you couldn't even imagine what it was like.

As a climax and final inducement, Raquel sent a magnificent present to my hotel with a note saying that he would be happy if he could just see me for an hour. The present was simply gorgeous. I could hardly get in the door. There stood six matched pieces of leather luggage. It was wonderful leather, and when I looked at it I saw the clasps and locks were made out of solid gold. There was also a jewel box that went with the set; it had my initials on it, and was also clasped and locked in gold. Since I was flying to New York that afternoon, I decided that I'd teach Raquel a lesson. I sent the jewel box back to him with a note (I paid the messenger enough to be sure he wouldn't steal the box). The note said: "I thought you were in love with me. How dare you send me this box empty?"

The results were a bit too much. Within half an hour Raquel himself was downstairs, telling me that an hour's conversation would fill the box to its brim. I told him I'd meet him that afternoon at three o'clock, and I took the two o'clock plane taking the luggage with me, as I thought that was the only fair thing to do.

That wasn't quite the end of Raquel, though. I found Junie, who had just come back herself, in the apartment, practically out of her head with excitement.

"Doris," she screamed, "I just got a message from the airport. They said that some man named Raquel had sent his plane here to take you back to Mexico!"

I called them, and told them that the whole thing was out of the question, and for them to tell the plane to go right home again.

When I came into the living room, Junie was absolutely popeyed. She had a remark for every occasion, but this once even Junie was stuck. All she could say was, "What a vacation! Doris, you certainly must have had a real good time."

CHAPTER 5

*I MEET SYBELLA,
OR THIRTY-THREE TIMES
AROUND THE ÉTOILE*

Like every traveler coming back, I expected that there would have been big changes in New York while I was away. Also like every traveler, I discovered that things were pretty much the same. Pretty much, I say: I detected a change in Junie. Whereas I had been the depressed one, she was now in a real low mood. The Southern trip hadn't done her any good—that I could see—but she wouldn't tell me why. She had fallen in love six times, she mentioned in passing, and was disillusioned six times. That was nothing new. She had had her head ground into the sand by the Florida surf. Thousands of people have.

The only clue she offered was a Virginia ham sandwich. When I would ask her, "Junie, why is it you are depressed?" she kept saying, "We just stepped into this place one night, and I asked the man what was good, and he said, a Virginia ham sandwich, cured like they did it at home. Well, I bit into that thing. I have never had such a sensation. I do not think it is nice to palm off old leather saddles on unsuspecting Northerners between two slices of rye bread." I merely told her not to take it so hard. She said, "You have never eaten one."

Then she took to staring at my luggage. It was something to stare at, I will admit, but not for hours, not evening after evening, especially when it was Junie, who did not care much about material possessions. I knew if I waited long enough she would finally tell me what was preying on her mind. And sure enough, one evening she was staring, I was dressing to go out; I turned to her and asked her, "Pigeon, what is it?" and she burst into tears and said, "Teeth!"

It took me a while to get the story straightened out. First I figured she had become enamored of a man, and then found out his teeth were not his own but those of a dentist. No, it was her own teeth she was talking about. When she had bitten into the Virginia ham sandwich she felt a sharp pain, which would not leave her. Back in the city, her dentist had told her that she needed a great many fillings. As usual, Junie had spent all her money (on monogrammed Italian underwear, which is not good to eat, nor will it do much for buttressing a molar). "Don't worry yourself," I said, "we will find a way." "I think I've got one," she answered. "What?" I asked. "Doris, honey," she said, her lips trembling, "could we melt down the solid gold locks on your luggage to make fillings for my teeth?"

Goodness knows I was willing. Junie, however, felt so much better getting things off her chest that she decided to go out again instead of spending her night staring. Within a matter of days, she had met a man who was best friends with a man who was one of America's leading dentists, and Junie's fillings were made from his dental Fort Knox, not my luggage locks.

Fortunately, too—because I was going to need that luggage. There was one other thing that made New York only pretty much the same. When I am at a party or a night club or on a country week end, people are not liable to confuse me conversationally with either Beatrice Lillie or the reincarnation of Madame Curie, yet I am not a silent Idiot Gertrude either. Whatever way the talk drifts, I have always felt that I can hold my own, and my listeners' complaints have never been too bitter. But after returning from Mexico, I found that for the first time conversation was out of control.

I would see people I thought I knew, and they would say, "Hello, Doris." That took about two seconds. Then for five hours they would say, "Cannes, Biarritz, Monte Carlo, *bistro, couturier*, Maxim's, Tour d'Argent, *fiacre, pourboire*, Left Bank." Between these words, there were long sentences that began, "Do you remember, before the war, Fritzie and I were driving through Arles..." and led through remembrances that left everyone foggy with nostalgia or weak with laughter. Those remembrances left me racked with yawns. I began to see that a whole group of Americans had been marking time, hanging around the provinces, such as New York City, crossing dates off their calendars till they could get Back To Europe. Not Over To Europe. Back.

It got to the pitch where when a man would turn to me and open his mouth as if to say something, I would say quickly, "Sorry, I haven't been there." Whereupon he would turn away, leaving me to count the charms on my bracelet, or the number of times the same thing had happened to me. I got so I finally would say, "Haven't been there before the war. I was too young." That happened to be the truth, but a great many women became hostile to me.

I have no idea exactly how hostile they might have gotten, because about then they all rushed onto boats and planes and left New York deserted. There were plenty of people still walking around the streets, but you wouldn't especially care to take those types *off* the streets. I mean, almost everybody I knew had gone. Back, of course.

There was only one thing to do. One afternoon, it was nearly five o'clock I remember, I said to this nice man who owned the restaurant in which I happened to be having tea, "Well, let's see what this is all about." "What what is all about?" he asked me. "Europe," I told him, and left him clinging to his half-eaten English muffin.

That is the way I am. I do not believe in planning, I believe in action. I was taking action, I was going to Europe. The question was, where in Europe? Out on the pavement it was an aching, windy day. Somewhere warm, I decided, somewhere sunny, and I remembered all those people shouting about Biarritz and Cannes. It was the south of France for me! That being the case, I right away called a taxi, and wheeled myself off to my favorite department store. There I bought two lovely bathing suits, one black, one navy blue. This purchase put the seal on my plans. I had the equipment, I would have a trip to match.

Full of my new enthusiasm, I returned to the apartment and broke the news to Junie. She thought it was marvelous, until I got to the bathing suit part. "Show them to me," she said. I did. "In the south of France in those, you will look like not one, but two members of the Floradora Sextette," Junie told me. "Not even a bare midriff. It's Bikinis or nothing there. Save them for a local tea dance." I asked her how did she know, as she had never been to Europe. "I know," she answered, and went back to running her tongue gleefully over her new fillings.

When Junie said she knew, she knew, regardless of any evidence on the other side, so I did not argue about it. Later events proved she knew, all right—only not enough, that was all.

The next step was getting a passport. To get a passport you need a birth certificate, ten dollars, and a friend. Some people get stumped at this stage; they've got ten dollars and a certificate, it's the friend they can't dig up. Also I needed a French visa. I had a passport, had packed a light bag (feeling confident I could find the stuffings for a heavy trunk in Paris, France), and had booked passage on an airplane, leaving in a week. Then I was told that it took ten days to get a French visa. By luck the same man whom I'd left holding the English muffin had a friend in the State Department. I had my visa the following morning.

The one crimp in my general joy was having to leave Junie in New York. I had only just enough money saved up for my own expenses; she promised me though that she would join me in Europe as soon as she was able to save up some money of her own. Knowing Junie's habits made me wonder if she would ever see anything more of Europe than the foreign feature at the Paris movie theater near the Plaza. This same knowledge next made me wonder if she would get past the ticket window into that foreign feature. (I was wrong.)

So, one bleak morning in a pouring rain, Junie waved good-by to my taxi as it headed for Idlewild Airport. I must say that leaving from an airport depresses me—no singing, no champagne in the cabin, no party to go along. Should it be a party when it leaves New York, it has bogged down into a group resembling a gang of bald old men trading stories on how they lost their hair by the time the long trek to the airport is complete. But I had to make up for lost European time, and the plane was fast. I figured also that by passing up a boat trip I would be passing up days of listening to Americans wondering loud and long if that dear old café on the Left Bank was the same as it had been before the war. I just settled back in the taxi and thought about how wonderful modern science and transportation were. I realized it was a cliché, but I thought about it just the same, looking out from the Queensboro Bridge.

In the exact middle of the Queensboro Bridge the taxi broke down, which is what comes of thinking in clichés, I guess. Another car pushed us over across the bridge, where the taximan tried to get his car started again. He got a dull whine from the motor. There wasn't another taxi in sight, and I was waiting and dying. The taxi driver said he had a friend at a garage right nearby, and I could hire a car from him.

Three quarters of an hour later in the driving rain he and I transferred my five pieces of luggage (which is what my light bag had turned into) to a hired limousine. I had allowed myself three hours to make the airport, but it was getting close. I told the chauffeur to drive like mad. He drove like mad for about fifteen minutes, at which time he drove like mad through a deep mud puddle, which stalled the limousine completely. I leaped out of the back seat, not waiting to hear him tell me about his carburetor or whatever it was, flagged a passing private car, told the man I would pay him ten dollars to drive me the rest of the way to Idlewild, and made the plane by an eel's eyebrow. I still do not believe it was that much of a cliché.

The atmosphere on the plane was like that of a community sing which was a bad failure. The plane company makes nice arrangements, everybody has a designated seat, and gets a form telling what everyone else's name is. But on my trip, everyone acted like they hated each other. We flew along in icy silence, broken only by snorts of terror when the motor missed a beat, and the noises made by an Australian woman who was sick the whole trip without any pause whatsoever that I could notice. She was quite a woman. The company tried to make a big deal out of the free bottle of champagne they give you. This did not make any dent in the surly silence; we were all too busy remembering the cost of our tickets, figuring out the cost of overweight in baggage, and listening to those motors.

We stopped at Newfoundland in a blizzard so terrible that you had to hold on to a rope to get from the plane to the airport building. We took off in the same blizzard. I was not upset by that occurrence. I said to myself, "Doris, there is no use worrying. Not at this altitude."

Nor was there any cause for alarm—by early afternoon we landed at Orly Airport. Now, I am not going to try to describe Paris, because in the first place I don't know the city well enough (which is some admission for an American tourist, I find), and because in the second place too many famous authors have done it better than I possibly could (which is not bad in the admitting department either, for a writer). Still, I am a human being. If you've been to Paris and don't want to say anything at all about it, you're not human, you're an orangutan. A stupid orangutan.

The airport is like any other airport, people are standing in line, the planes' roar sounds over the stamp, stamp, stamp of the customs inspectors. The outskirts of the city are a disappointment. Paris is no exception to the rule that you usually enter a town by its worst-looking part. Paris itself is as beautiful as everyone has called it. Driving toward the center of the city to my hotel, the Plaza-Athénée, I of course noticed most of all the wide, tree-lined avenues, the blue-green bronze statues, and the thousands of little cars honking like crazy. No wonder they have to honk; there are absolutely no stop signals anywhere in Paris. Later on in my stay, I myself was driving one of those tiny foreign cars, when I found myself on the enormous traffic circle by the avenue Foch. About fifteen streets all empty onto the circle; cars were coming at me as fast and from as many directions as snowflakes. Every time I came to my avenue, I was too frightened to turn, and would go around the circle again. By actual count I drove around the circle thirty-three times in a panic; the thirty-fourth I gave a giant honk on the horn, closed my eyes, and shot into the avenue safely. To drive in Paris, you have to take the initiative: honk first, look later.

I thought I might as well start off my European jaunt with a bang. My residence in the Plaza-Athénée, one of the smartest hotels in Paris, was a four-room suite. I unpacked, roamed around my rooms, then wondered what to do. It is an awful thing to say that I wondered what to do my first evening in Paris. It is the truth. In my usual way, I had not written anyone I was coming, nor had I bothered to find out where my friends were staying. Eat, I thought, always a good first move. I got no farther with that project than the lobby.

There, luckily, I ran into a lobby bird, an outstanding type of American in Paris. He is the man who spends his whole day going from lobby to lobby. Once in a lobby he goes to the desk, barks out an order for a cable blank, then stands and peers around until he sees someone he knows coming in. This time it was me.

"Hello, Doris!" he bellowed. "When did you get in?

This afternoon? Did you know that Mona and Charlie are at the Whichwhat Hotel? and David is staying with the Beverleys in the rue Peculiar? And Franz and the Lang brothers have been at the Nonsense Hotel for two weeks?"

By the time he is finished, you know the exact location of every friend you have in town. Happy to have been seen talking with someone well-dressed and in their right mind, he goes on to another cable blank, another lobby, to report your whereabouts to any interested parties. His moment of glory comes when he bumps into a really well-known person, when the bellboys can report they've seen him telling Walter Pidgeon where his pals are (if French bellboys know who Walter Pidgeon is, and if they happen to be watching). However, the lobby bird is doing his best to be a useful citizen, and all he wastes is cable blanks and his own time.

That evening he must have sped to his next lookout post on winged, two-toned oxfords, because no sooner had I taken a few sips of my first *apéritif* when a troop of friends came in, waving and halloing. "We ran into Jeff," they explained unnecessarily. I told them it was awfully sweet of them to come all the way over to find me, but why, I wondered, hadn't they merely telephoned?

They all looked as if I'd asked them why they didn't stand with one foot in a bathtub full of water, while holding on to a naked piece of electrically charged wire. A girl I knew eventually pulled herself out of her horrified silence to explain the Paris telephone to me.

"Don't use it," she said, "unless you want to have a fast case of the screams. If you have to use it, practice saying the number you want to get, over and over, till you can say it fast. Then get down in a crouch, run around the room three or four times to get up speed, hurl yourself on the phone, and shout it out like a tobacco auctioneer. You'll get the wrong one. Try again four times. Then send someone out with a note." I still didn't understand. "Why so fast?" I inquired. "If you want Elysée 2311," she told me, "and you say it normally, the operator will maybe let you get as far as Elysée 23 if you're shot with luck, and she'll connect you with that. Sometimes it's just Elysée 2. Once I got as far as Elysée. I'll never know how *that* happened."

How right she was! Three nights later, I was out with a charming Frenchman who had to make a business call to Nice. After getting two towns in Switzerland and a Left Bank café, he gave up. He got into his private plane, flew to Nice, transacted his business, and was back in Paris while the operator was still busy. On his return he found she'd connected him with a perfectly charming restaurant in Marseilles. Yet with all its drawbacks, I found that the French telephone plays a large role in the lives of two classes of people in Europe: a certain kind of American, and the International Woman.

Anyway, my friends wouldn't hear of my dining alone in a hotel. So my first night in Paris I spent in its most celebrated restaurant-night club, Maxim's. Maxim's isn't like a New York night club, either West or East Side—it's something like both, and it's got qualities all its very own. Like a West Side place, it's big, there's room for lots of people, and like a West Side spot, the crowd is very mixed—women in *couturier* gowns rub elbows with shop girls, bankers jostle against men who live mostly on racetrack bets. Like an East Side club, the headwaiter is king of the place, and as in the Stork or El Morocco, the customers are busy as bee-stung firemen checking up on each other. You're stared at every minute.

But mostly Maxim's is like itself, not like New York places. One of the things I noticed first was the lighting. It was like a clear night on the desert. Stark. No peering through the gloom here—everyone in the room stands out like a glowworm. No gewgaws on the tables; no little lamps, no souvenirs, no cards, no bottles of perfume. Then you have to call it a restaurant-night club because, though there's an orchestra and a dance floor, the food is just as important as in a place devoted solely to it. I have always said that I thought there were two ideal deaths for a playboy—to drop dead while doing a samba, or to be burnt to a cinder by the flames under the *crêpes Suzette*. In Maxim's he had his choice.

I found out the reason for the mixed crowd. In Paris there is no café society. There is society, and there are people who go to night clubs. Here, anyone with the price of a meal is welcome; the headwaiter seats you according to how attractive you are, not how important. If you present yourself there for the first time, beautifully dressed, with a handsome man, you'll be given a wonderful table, even if you are the garbage collector's niece and the man with you is the dogcatcher.

However, Paris *is* headquarters for a kind of café

society, the International Set. They resemble the home team by being made up of nearly every type—demimondaines wearing few or many diamond bracelets according to how good they are in their profession, Russian dukes and counts, Americans who spend as much time abroad as they do in their own country, Swiss, Belgians, English—it's a boiling melting pot.

But boiling. The International Set is distinguished for its stamina. It makes café society look like a bunch of loafers. For instance, there is one man. Nobody knows how he lives, but he's living. He has a country estate, a fabulous town apartment, yachts (which he sometimes sells twice; nobody minds, he is so charming). He tips enormously, he's always everywhere, and he's far from young. Well, one morning that man woke up and he couldn't move a muscle, not a muscle. He'd had a stroke, the doctor told him, and he wasn't going out dancing that night or any night for about five years. After the doctor left, the man called his valet and told him to bring a bottle of vodka to his bedside. He drank the entire bottle of vodka, then dragged himself painfully to the edge of the pool (which was a side feature of his flat), flopped into the icy water, stayed under half a minute, and came up laughing. That night he was the rage of the dance floor and he is to this day.

Still and all, he was a slug-a-bed when compared to the International Woman. She would have jumped up without vodka or swimming pool, because she wouldn't have had the stroke in the first place, someone else would. That's the way she is. The International Woman is European, though she may now live in America.

She's got an accent, well preserved. She is usually on the cloudy side of forty, though she can be young. Her hair is pretty generally bottled red, her fingernails long and likewise—and believe me, she knows how to use them. She favors a combination of clothes such as a turquoise-blue dress with a blaring pink hat, with touches of green here and there on the costume. Many times she has a title, married somewhere along the line, or invented out of her own cozy little imagination.

Americans hear of American girls who go over to Europe to marry titles. That might have been true in days gone by, but now it's the International Woman out to marry the American man. She recognizes one title, Cash; and it's perfectly all right with her if her crest is a simple old dollar sign.

I did not find all this out at once. I wish I had. I learned by slow, bitter experience, starting my first night in Maxim's. Immediately after dinner, Sybella bore down on us. She looked exactly like a fire engine—red hair, red dress covered with silver birds that looked like a fire truck's chrome trim, and instead of a siren, she kept sounding her "Darleeng, darleeng," at regular intervals, so the smaller vehicles could get out of her way before being flattened.

"Darleeng," she sounded at the girl who had explained the Paris phone to me, "how sweet you look tonight!" That girl froze up as if she had seen an adder. I saw why, because Sybella then shouted, "Sweeet, sweeet, just like a leetle dairymaid out of the farm. Ah, Mees Leelly, I am Countess Sybella von Toade. My deear, how attractive you are. But that hair! Why do you wear it back? So old! And those eyebrows! Too heavy! We must pluck them. Come to see me tomorrow. We weel find you some prettier clothes than that! You cannot stay in Paris now! No one is here. You weel motor to Cannes with me in a week. Yes, it is all arranged."

And it was. I never knew what struck me. At first I thought maybe she really wanted to help me, I thought maybe she really meant those things in a kind way. Anyway, hot or cold, I was to meet her the next day at her apartment, and she was going to take me shopping at her own *couturier's!* I was thrilled, I must say. Instead of being thrilled I should have gone over to the nearest zoo and locked myself in with the tigers. That way I would have come to less harm.

Next morning I took a long time getting dressed, so I would live up to Sybella's standards. (I never thought of that awful red dress—it was her gall she wore, not clothes really, and her gall was twenty-four carat, the genuine article.) I must confess I even plucked my eyebrows.

The servant showed me into Sybella's bedroom. She was still in bed, holding the phone. "Darleeng, we are delayed. I have put through an important phone call, and also I am expecting a cable." The International Woman would as soon appear without her phone call as she would without her lightning sense of addition. I can say no more than that. At sea, on land, in the wilderness, she has put through her call and is expecting her cable. For months I believed in these calls and cables, until one time when a group of us were in a little town in France, waiting, because the local International Woman had put through a long distance call. Finally one of the men got so tired of waiting that he checked up with the operator, who informed him that no long-distance call had been put in from that town for two years, when an American movie company on location there had rung up Paris. By then I had learned enough about her not to be surprised. A good 90 per cent of the International Woman consists of props.

A big prop was jewelry. Finishing her dressing after a cool three hours, Sybella called, "My jewels, my jewels, breeng me my jewels." The maid ran out of the room, came back with boxes, cases, piles of chamois bags, and we spent another two hours deciding between the emeralds and the diamonds-and-rubies. Sybella was one of the most successful of the International Women. All her jewels were real. Other International Women, not as well heeled, buy one large piece of jewelry, authentic, and fill in the gaps with zircons. But they call for their zircons in the same voice of authority that Sybella used calling for her emeralds.

Sybella, finally dressed, sailed out the door, flashing, sparkling, screaming, gay in blue and yellow, with plumes. She, the chauffeur, two poodles, and I squeezed into what she called "My leetle, leetle runabout car." The leetle, leetle runabout, plus a closed car and a limousine, had been magnetized out of a middle-aged American representing Bend-Pruf Plastics in Europe. The plastic may have been bend-proof, but he ran like wax under Sybella's charm and strength.

After a short but hair-raising ride, the leetle, leetle

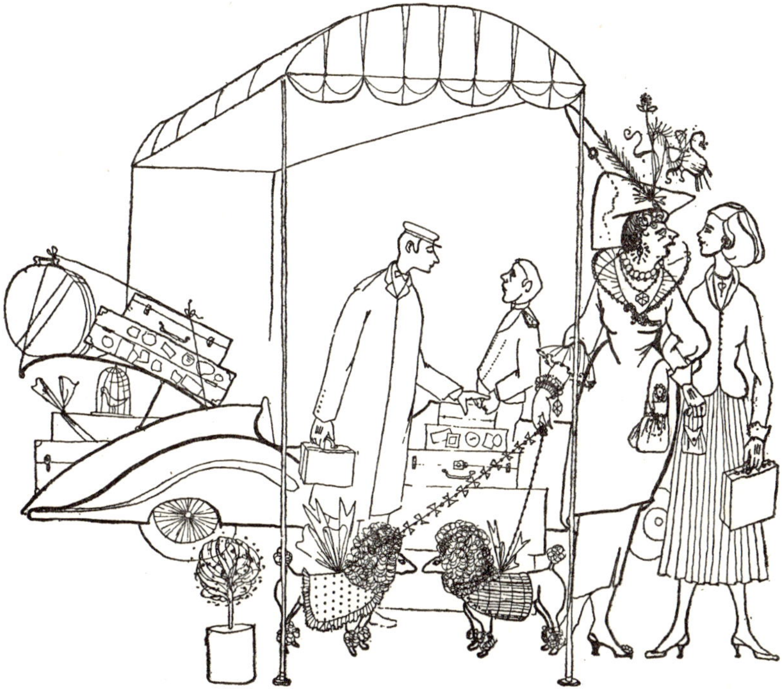

unabout pulled up in front of the *couturier's*. Once inside, we were ushered into a large room, filled with rickety gilt chairs all facing toward a raised platform. Sybella sprinkled greetings around like sand, and under cover of her wavings and darleengs pushed herself into the second row, where her plumes blocked the vision of five women behind her, and her comments prevented them from hearing anything else that was said.

Now by nature I am strictly a Lord & Taylor girl. I go in, I try on, I buy a dress, or say I'll be back. I have never been persecuted for this practice. It's American. I'm used to it. Here, I could see, was a different situation altogether. A silver pencil was dropped in my hand, I was given a card with a list of the names of the dresses to be shown, each name with a number beside it. All in French, naturally. Then a girl walked onto the platform, called the name of her dress out in mushy French, and stalked off. It was then I found that the dresses were not shown in the order they were listed. All around me women were making important notes after the names of the models, and checking others. Sybella checked more and made more notes than anyone I could see. I strained my ears trying to catch the names, but I didn't make any headway, and spent the rest of the time trying to figure out how many dollars are in one hundred thousand francs, making a few notes and checks on my card just to get into the act.

I must have looked at one hundred and thirty-five models that afternoon, with what I hoped was passing for an expression of expert interest. At the end of the ordeal, I was looking forward only to my hotel and a hot bath. The dresses I liked I couldn't remember the names of, and the names I remembered didn't connect with any dresses. I started to thank Sybella and make my escape, when she cried, "But here is my *own vendeuse*."

Her own *vendeuse* (salesgirl to the peons) was bending over me with the expression of a vulture who has just sighted an overturned truck marked "Swift & Armour." She in turn summoned another attendant dressed like a Roxy usherette, who whisked me into a dressing room, where the *vendeuse* snatched from my hand my neat little card full of straggly checks and my attempts to figure out how many dollars are in one hundred thousand francs.

The events of the afternoon had reduced me to the point where I couldn't remember even the few phrases of French I knew. The Roxy usherette was forced to indicate by sign language that I was to take off my dress so I could try on the clothes models they were bringing in. She held my dress between her thumb and finger and hung it up in a dim corner as if she had found some dead insect around and wanted to hide it. This, naturally, made me feel even lower and more nervous than I felt already.

"Anyway," I thought, looking in the mirror with some pride, "my underwear is pretty. They can't sneer at that." My mother always told me to wear my best underwear when going out, especially in cities where the traffic was heavy. "What if you get run over, Doris?" she would say. "You wouldn't want a lot of strangers to see you in underwear that wasn't nice."

Just then the *vendeuse* came back. By means of a ouija board, or a quick tea-leaf reading, she had decided my doodles meant that I wanted two ball gowns and a gray *tailleur,* or suit. She took a look at me standing in my underwear, and from the glances she and the usherette gave each other, I could see that it might as well have had "Inferior Grade Flour" stamped all over it. Overcoming their disgust, they put the first ball gown on me, and called for a third helper, who appeared with a tape measure, pins, and a notebook. The ball gown was pale pink; it had a pouffe here, a tuck there, a little train, a folded neckline, and I felt like the Queen of the May in it.

I turned around, and I guess I was looking awfully happy and preening in the mirror, when the third helper whipped the tape measure around my waist. I turned to her, smiling. She looked at me with horrified eyes, and let out a groan. Then she said some number of centimeters to the other two, and they groaned with her. The *vendeuse* not only groaned, she put her head in her hands. The third attendant, or witch, as I began to think of her, then measured my shoulders. The number of centimeters in my shoulders made her sob. My back made her wince; when she measured my hips, the result was so terrible that the usherette had to leave the fitting room temporarily. I didn't dare look at myself in the second ball gown. When we got to the *tailleur,* I wasn't sure if I felt more like Gorgeous George or a badly made telegraph pole, with lumps.

In America, I usually got a size twelve, without alterations. From the gestures that went with the French spitting back and forth between the *vendeuse* and the measuring witch, I gathered that in France, I wasn't merely out, I was out altogether. Where had I picked up those muscles? (I hadn't seen any muscles before, but glancing quickly into the mirror I thought I saw them, great big rippling ones, across my back.) Why was my waist so long? How come my hips were constructed the way they were? At the end of an hour, I realized that only the bigheartedness of this particular *maison de couture* permitted them to even consider making clothes for a monster like me.

With tears of gratitude and shame in my eyes, I thanked the *vendeuse* and the measuring witch, put my rag (as I now thought of my dress) on my misshapen form, and limped back to the hotel. It was a whole week before I could walk out into the street without shuddering at my own boldness. For two days I wouldn't go out in the daylight at all. I would wait until nighttime, when my awful imperfections wouldn't show up so clearly.

And so I found out how many dollars there are in one hundred thousand francs.

With Sybella at the reins, the rest of my stay in Paris was a blur. I was always going somewhere, or leaving somewhere, or expected somewhere. I felt like a mouse in an egg beater; nevertheless I suppose I did most of the things that every tourist in Paris does.

I had a meal in a restaurant that was purely, solely a restaurant, dedicated to food like a shrine is to a saint. The atmosphere made a tomb seem noisy. The air was gray; around me were a lot of Frenchmen eating slowly, silently, with the rapt expression of Dodger fans. The food was magnificent, but I can't say I felt easy. Still, I tried to copy their facial reserve; I pretended I was comfortable wedged into a tiny table, which I practically knocked over each time I crossed my legs. (As I have said, I am tall; I am tall for an American, but in the Parisian scale of things, mothers pointed me out to their children as a new Eiffel Tower.) I took as long to eat as anyone in the room, wheezed joyously over the wine, and generally made myself as silly as Americans do pretending that they are familiar with French ways.

I was taken to the romantic French night club. I had heard that each table was covered with roses, that there were only violins in the orchestra, that one could drink nothing but champagne served out of silver goblets. Naturally I was all for checking into the club, sight unseen, and making it my second home. "How wonderful it will be," I told the American who was taking me there, "What a change from rough and ready American manners! Romance, old world charm, a touch of the past when ladies leaned out of castle windows waving farewell to their knights!" He agreed, nervously adjusting his collar; I could see he was a trifle scared that he would not live up to the surroundings. Truthfully, so was I.

When we got there, it was all as advertised, roses, violins, champagne on each table. My first difficulty was with the roses. The table here was as small as in the other restaurant, and in order to keep it from rising on my knees, I had to lean on it with my elbows. Every time I leaned an elbow I would strike a thorn. The waiters passed the word around to watch me, I was epileptic. Then the violins—in America, you pay violinists to play at your table. The Europeans do it more shrewdly. The violinists, all fifteen of them, clustered around our table, and played for dear life. At first my escort and I pretended we thought it was divine. My hairdo was blown all out of shape by the breeze they were creating, and I saw that he was turning pale from the noise, so I yelled, "Send them away!" He waved a feeble hand. The noise grew louder. We began to feel that we were inside a violin. He shooed them away again, more violently. They played louder. In desperation he reached in his pocket (he had already given them some money) and gave them more money. The racket stopped like magic.

So remember, in Europe, you pay the violinist to go away. It took the rest of the evening for the pounding in our ears to go away, too.

There was still the champagne. Silver goblets were brought to us, a cork popped (I saw it pop, though I couldn't hear it), and after raising our goblets in a toast, we drank. Ah, I thought, the silver cups are beautiful; such luxury, the exotic ringing in our ears, this place, this wine. Did you ever take a bite of a chocolate bar and get a piece of the tinsel paper lodged in your teeth? Exactly the same feeling. Short of eating the can with the sardine, there is nothing like it. I fell into bed at the Plaza-Athénée, shattered, just shattered, emotionally and physically.

But the following day, the sun was shining; it was

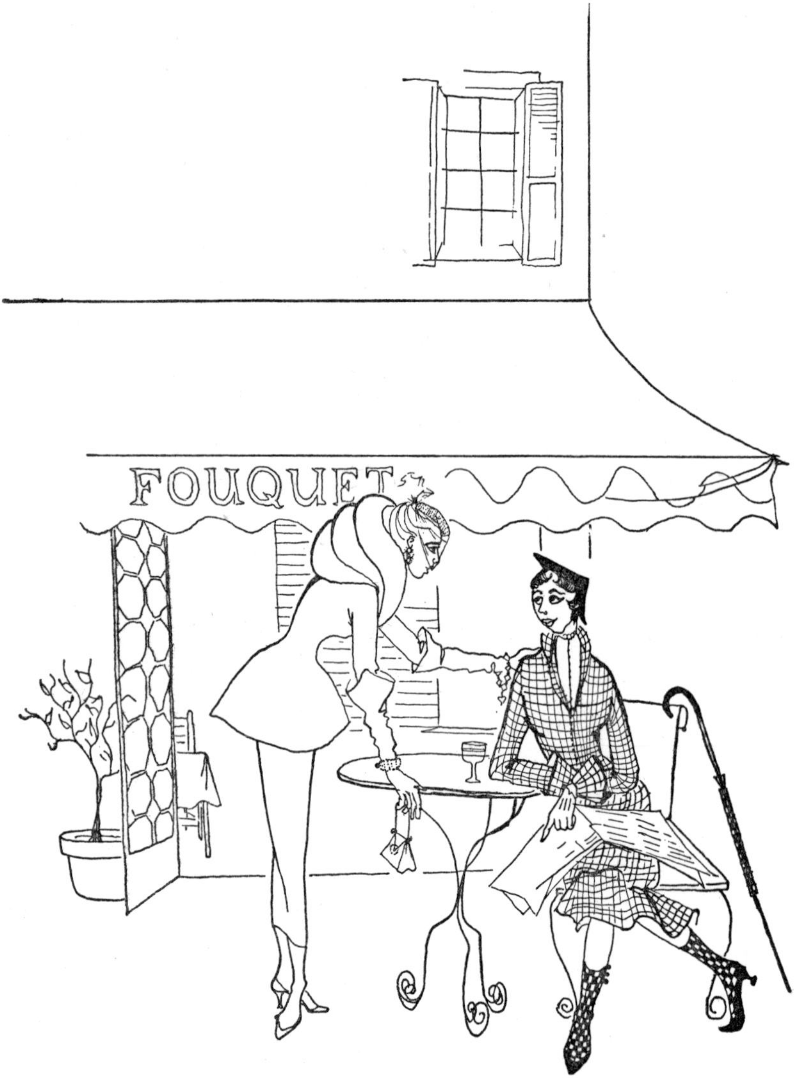
FOUQUET

too lovely out to be feeling real depressed. I gave Sybella the slip (she wanted me to go to her *own boutique* and pick up some leetle handbags. I hinted there was no use in a handbag unless you had a leetle something to put in it, and pretended our telephone connection had been broken). In all the rush and confusion, I hadn't even had a chance to stroll around Paris, so I set off along the Champs Elysées, looking at the crowds and listening to their chatter.

At the corner of the Champs Elysées and the avenue Georges V is Fouquet's, with one of the largest sidewalk cafés in Paris. Feeling thirsty, I dropped in to get a glass of something cold. While I sat there sipping, my eye fell on a girl three tables away. "A true Parisienne," I thought enviously. And she *was*, the American's idea of the Paris woman: tricorne hat set rakishly on her head, close fitting, narrow shouldered black and white checked suit, severe linen blouse, black patent leather opera pumps, and as the perfect last touch, a pair of matching checkered gaiters over her instep. She was reading a French newspaper. She lowered it, I saw her face, and spilled my drink all over the table and my own lap. "Junie!" I screamed.

"'allo," said Junie.

"What do you mean, 'allo?" I asked. "Come on, it's me, Doris!"

"Eets nice to see you, Dorees," said Junie.

"'Eet's nice,' my foot," I yelped, "what's the matter with you?"

"Oh shut up," said Junie. "Can't I have a little fun pretending I'm French?"

"I'm sorry," I told her. "It was such a shock seeing you."

That soothed her down. I had another fruit drink, she had another *fine*, which is all she would drink, regardless of the hour of day, and she told me developments. "How long are you here for?" I asked her. "Three days," she said. "Three days! Why only that?" I wondered.

"I have finally met a man who owns *everything*," Junie said. And from the sound of it, he did—oil wells, airplane companies, real estate firms, silver mines. "So it was no trouble for him to get me over here. What the trouble is," Junie added, "is he likes me too much, and he figures if he lets me stay over here for more than three days, I won't come back for a long time, maybe years. In which he is so right. I don't know when I have liked a town so much. Then I have got to get back to see about the house."

"What house?" I asked her, more puzzled than ever.

"Well, one evening he asked me, couldn't he get me a nice present of some kind," said Junie. "Now, Doris, I truly love this man, so I said no, I didn't want a present. Not unless it was something we could both enjoy, like a little town house where I could cook him a dinner and he could relax. So he is fixing up this little town house and I have to see about it."

I told Junie I had always known she was a thoughtful person. She agreed with me. Then she explained how she had got in that morning, bought herself the suit, the hat, the shoes, and the gaiters ("Gosh, those gaiters," she said, lifting up one foot), and had been playing French ever since.

Junie sure wanted to see Paris night life; so we fixed it up that Sybella and I and three men I had met in Paris would pick her up at her hotel that evening. She was staying over on the Left Bank somewhere. "Nothing but a bunch of tourists over here," she said, picking up her newspaper again. I was merely grateful she wasn't reading it upside down.

When we came by for her, she had another little black hat, a low-cut black wool dress, and she had managed to part with the gaiters. "It was tough," she whispered to me. Sybella gave her the full treatment, or hosing—telling her she looked so charming, but so short, my dear, wasn't it a peety, and the chin was so long, no two ways about it.

"That woman is a dirty skunk," Junie said, and didn't speak a word to Sybella all evening. I told her she was being nasty; she wouldn't listen to it.

We went to the opening of a Left Bank *cave*, supposedly pronounced with an open-wide "ah," but you can give it the New York "a" and be closer to the truth. Low, dirty, crammed with uncouth types, all the women going to the men's room, an orchestra playing what they thought was the latest American hot music (Louis Armstrong, 1938), and some bathless Griselda baritoning out songs from a barstool.

Junie almost lost her mind over the place. "So French, so French," she kept saying. I liked it myself. Don't ask me why. Maybe it was because of my poet. Like some people acquire a dog or a cat, during my stay in

Paris, I got myself a poet. It wasn't anything the way it sounds, and it happened like this:

One evening an escort and I were in a Left Bank place, a lot like the one I was showing Junie, when I saw, over in the corner, a wretched-looking creature. He was covered with grime, his sweater was a menu of all he had eaten over two months, and he was absolutely the homeliest thing in the world. Still, there was something fascinating about him. I learned that he was a famous French poet, which explained a lot. Back in Santa Monica I had been told that poets were a pretty dirty gang, and that you had to expect them to be peculiar. Anyway, this Marcel and I got talking (he spoke English), and I'll say for him that he could talk real well. I liked his conversation, and what is more, I pitied him. He was hungry all the time, never had enough to eat. In fact he was so hungry sometimes that he could hardly open a door.

So I got in the habit of giving him five hundred francs a day. No matter where I would be of an evening, I would make the man with me take me over to the Left Bank. I would look around the ant-hill-type bistros till I found Marcel and gave him the money. It was five hundred francs, because Marcel lived strictly for the moment. If I gave him a thousand, he'd spend it right then and there, and not have enough for breakfast. I felt awfully good about it, but it took Junie to put it into words.

Marcel came to the *cave* opening, and talked to Junie and me. She couldn't speak for the glamour of it all. I gave him his five hundred francs; after he had gone I told Junie how I was helping him, and she looked at me and said, "Doris, you are a patron of the arts." Come to think of it, I guess I was at that."

The following two days I showed Junie all the places I had found in Paris. We had ourselves a bang-up time. Then she had to go back to the town house (she said she'd sublet the apartment, that I'd be coming home to a mansion, not just a tacky old flat).

She wasn't the only one who had to leave. Sybella had been champing at the bit; she announced that she wouldn't stay another minute in Paris, darleeng, it was empty, positively, we *had* to go on to Cannes.

We motored to Cannes in the leetle, leetle runabout, complete with baggage, chauffeur, and most of all, Sybella. Oh, I nearly forgot the dogs. I will never know what the scenery is like between Paris and Cannes—all I saw the entire trip was the black nose and small eyes of Chou-Chou, the elder of Sybella's two poodles.

CHAPTER 6

THE RIVIERA IS FOR PENGUINS

CANNES ITSELF LOOKS LIKE ALMOST ANY seaside resort when you pull into it. It could be Atlantic Beach—with trees. It could be Santa Monica—with trees. A couple of things make it outstanding. One is the color of the sea. You have never seen anything like it. Sometimes it is phosphorus green, sometimes a real Kelly green, and at twilight, when the sun is going down, it turns the color of blue ink, deep blue with a band of yellow thrown over it from the setting sun. The other thing is the people. You could take half a lifetime talking about the people in Cannes, and you still wouldn't have it. The best I can do is try to strike some high lights.

They are such a mixture. There are Greeks, Levantines, Egyptians, White Russians, Englishmen, Dutch, Belgians, Spaniards, Americans, South Americans—even some Frenchmen. There are a whole lot of types so mixed up with different nationalities that there isn't any single name you could call them. They are rich, they are poor; young, old, and in between. They are quiet, loud, sporty, dull. Some of them are bouncing around like yoyos; some of them never make a move if they can help it. Cannes reminded me of a tank in a pet shop window jammed with all kinds of fish. Except that in the fish tank at least everything is a fish. In Cannes you couldn't really be sure if all the people were really even people.

But I waded right in with the best of them. I was back on the track of millionaires, and I wasn't going to be put off just because they looked sort of odd to me. In Paris I had been a tourist. I was going out to the best places with real important people, but my heart wasn't in that part of it so much. At the time I wanted to give all my attention to Paris itself. Furthermore, there was always Sybella to nudge me in the ribs if my eye wandered to a man during the evening. If she told me once, she told me constantly that Paris was a ghost town. According to her, everybody who was really rich, famous, or good looking was on the Riviera. Well, now we had made the Riviera. I was going to get my first taste of a European millionaire. To tell you the truth, I was straining at the leash.

Sybella naturally wasn't paying for any room and board. She was staying with friends—her friends. She as much as told me that I wasn't quite good enough to fit in with them, and advised me to put myself up at what she called the only hotel in Cannes—the Carlton.

The people at Cannes were my first shock; that hotel was sure my second. What a place! It was simply out of this world. Intrigue! It's a wonder to me the whole place didn't fly off its basement. I have never in all my life heard so much scuttling around and charging up and down, so many fights, so many makings-up, so many plans and appointments and general nonsense. It didn't take me an hour to see that there is something special in the air on the Riviera. I don't know exactly what it is, but it's there. I saw it right off. You might say it was the spirit of adventure, if you wanted to be fancy about it. Fiancés leave each other, lovers stalk off in opposite directions, wives leave their husbands, husbands desert their wives—but it's all in fun. It's madness; everyone there lives that way. It's today that counts; tomorrow can drop dead.

On account of the prevailing spirit of adventure the elevators in that hotel were covered with cobwebs. The stair carpeting, on the other hand, had to be replaced every few weeks so many people were sneaking up and down from floor to floor. Another sensational feature of the hotel was its design. It was built in the shape of a deep, narrow horseshoe, with the lobby in the front and big wings reaching back. Though I had a middle inside room, I didn't see what it all meant until I was dressing to go out.

"Hey, Jack," said a man's voice from the window next to mine. "Middle row of windows, third from the top."

"God Almighty," answered a voice I guessed belonged to Jack.

I stuck my head out of my own windows and saw two

guys in the next two rooms leaning out of their windows, each with a pair of binoculars glued to his eyes. Looking across the way, I immediately saw why. It was getting dark; lights had gone on. In many cases shades had not been drawn. I quickly pulled my head in from an over-all view that made me feel like a greenhorn fresh out of Nasty, Nebraska. I will not say that on following evenings I did not occasionally sneak a look. I am not made of stone.

What I was dressing for was a *gala*. As I, like many Americans, wasn't too sure what a gala was, Sybella had explained it to me. Rubbing in my ignorance with every word, need I say? With a few exceptions there are no night clubs around the Riviera. What it's got instead are big gambling casinos. The main part of the casino is for gambling; one room is called the night club, and often there is a terrace for outdoor drinking and dancing. One night of the week is gala night—a sort of party run on the same principle as a benefit is in this country. Except that I got the idea that the only thing that benefited was the casino. You call up for a reservation, and they charge as much as the traffic will bear. People go in groups, dressed in evening clothes. They watch the entertainment, they dance, gamble, and generally enjoy themselves. If the weather is lovely, a gala is usually held outside on the terrace. This is how Sybella explained it to me. It sounded like the kind of thing I had dreamed about, back at Santa Monica community dances, and wild horses couldn't have kept me away. I should have known Sybella would leave out a few piddling details, like the heart of the whole idea.

Most of my luggage, including my two ball gowns, hadn't arrived yet from Paris. Remembering the fashion magazine advice, I decided to wear a "little black dress"—a full black linen skirt with a turtle-necked black blouse and my pearls. Sure that I would get by even if I wasn't the fanciest dressed woman in the room, I took a taxi to the casino where I was to meet Sybella and her party.

In my life there have been many stunning moments—moments when I could only ask, "Floor, why don't you open?" But this moment, *this* moment, made all the rest look like happy birthday parties.

Sybella's getup was really something. On her it did not look its best; but on anyone, anywhere, it would have been a real sensational dress. It was the color of an apricot, satin, down in front, way down in back, all over crystal beading so fine some seamstress must have gone blind making it. It looked as if she had nearly emptied the boxes and the chamois bags. I had to throw one arm over my eyes to prevent an instant case of jewelry blindness. Sybella switched her train around and started off on me:

"Darleeng, my deear, this is your idea of what to wear to a gala? Too saad. Never mind, no one will notice, probably. They weel say you did not understand," and on like that until we got to our table. On the way I passed the best of Dior, Fath, Maggy Rouff, Schiaparelli, Grès, Heaven knows what. Each woman was bent double under the weight of diamonds, pearls, rubies, emeralds, sapphires. The heart of a gala is that it's a dressing contest. This one was fierce. I felt like a chimney sweep whom the duke has asked into the manorial hall for a Christmas drink.

It would be nice to say that in spite of her dress all eyes turned to Cinderella Lilly and she was the hit of the ball; it would be nice, but it would not be true. I was the lost chord of the ball. Flop would be too soft a word for what I was. Instead of looking for the best millionaires, I was looking for the best hiding places. I was in a state of shock and nerves. But a few items did manage to get in past the mist.

It was all the wrong way around. Men were working away for dear life at how to meet a millionairess. Not all of them but a lot of them. The way they eyed the women's jewels you expected them to whip out jewelers' glasses and give them a real appraisal. They were in corners humming about how Glorianna Glunk's father's investments had turned out. Young attractive men couldn't take their eyes off grisly women of a well-preserved one hundred and four years. They couldn't seem to stop whispering in their ears either. I was almost flattened by repulsion.

One of the boys even trapped me. Maybe thinking my little black dress was a new dodge for avoiding him and his type, he pushed a finger under my necklace, smiled with all his bicuspids, and asked, "Are your pearls real?"

I saw spots. He didn't see my eyes or think I had a nice profile or an interesting smile—no, just those pearls.

So I said to him, "The only way you can tell if pearls are real is to bite them. To bite them you must have real teeth. So you will never know if these pearls are the McCoy or from the five and dime."

It was a shot in the dark, but what a shot! He closed his mouth with a click—two clicks, one for the upper set, one for the lower—and barged away. That man's teeth were as false as his ideals, and everyone knew it. That was also my only triumph of the evening. Everything else was sheer humiliation, humiliation, humiliation.

I told myself that it didn't matter, that most of the men there probably didn't count for much anyhow. Later I saw that I had been pretty much on the right track when I thought that.

Later wasn't that night though, and it couldn't make up for what the fireworks did to me. Besides everything else, there is entertainment at a gala. At this gala they had a dance team, some singers, and a magician. They would run up the steps onto the terrace looking as if they had come out of the sea. Then they would go into their routines. The lights were so blazing that the night sky looked like a black curtain behind them. I had to admit it was pretty terrific.

As the high spot of the entertainment they set off fireworks. Which would have been great, except that the French, always eager to do things in a different way, pushed their enthusiasm a notch too far. The fireworks were supposed to look as if they were coming up out of the sea, too. And they did. But the people who were setting them off couldn't see where they were landing or didn't know what they were doing, because rockets and shooting stars and Roman candles kept coming near the dance floor and the table cloths and the bar. The fur stole of one old glamour girl caught fire from the sparks, and for a while it looked like we'd have roast baroness for the next course. There was almost a panic. The gigolos lost their toupees in the rush for the exits. Anyway, I suppose I shouldn't have been laughing so hard; a rocket came sailing down near me, and before I knew what had happened, there was an eight-inch hole in the back of my black linen skirt. Even if it served me right for laughing, it was the end. I tore out of the place as if a dinosaur were after me.

It was an evening from which I gained nothing. No fun, no compliments, no millionaires—nothing. Except I was on to Countess Sybella von Toade at last. Any woman who would do the thing she had to a girl like me who meant her no harm was too ruthless to fool around with. She could stay with her friends—that was fine by me. I was getting out from under her barbed-wire wing. What did I need with her? I figured that there must be plenty of ways to meet people besides having her introduce me to them.

Between the trip, the humiliation, the Comte de False Teeth, and the fireworks, it was the middle of the next afternoon before I woke up. I put on a nice beach dress, and as a gesture of defiance my pearls, and went downstairs in search of a sandwich and a cup of coffee. At the desk I found I had slept through four of Sybella's phone calls; she had left four messages. I merely dropped them into the most convenient waste basket. "Today it's a solo," I thought. "No dual controls for Doris."

Over coffee and a sandwich in the beach bar I drew the waiter into conversation. Why, yes, there certainly was a gathering place, he said. It was right in this hotel.

If you weren't there at the cocktail hour, you simply weren't on the Riviera—that was all. I thanked him and dashed upstairs again. By seven, I was in my summer cocktail-hour rig and all set to go. To be sure, I hadn't been properly introduced to many people at Cannes, but the chances were I would run into someone I knew down in the bar. And who knows? Maybe people would welcome a new friend, even if she hadn't been properly introduced.

I didn't have to ask where the bar was. I could hear where it was. There was a roaring and a laughing and a general bellow. I followed the sound outside to an enormous terrace and got mixed up with what I was sure for a couple of minutes was a cattle stampede. If Roy Rogers had appeared on Trigger riding herd it wouldn't have surprised me one little bit.

When I say that terrace was big, it really was big, believe me, and there wasn't an empty table on it. People were piled around the tables like pigeons around a bag of popcorn. People were standing up in the spaces between tables, milling around from one to the other, looking for a place to sit, and waving at each other. More people were waiting to get in just to mill around with the standees. The flashiest cars in the world were stalled for blocks around bringing more and more people to the Carlton Terrace. You'd think they were giving away gold dust on the inside, the way the crowd was pushing and shoving. I gave one great big shove and found myself in an aisle being carried along with the tide. I was swept clear from one end of the terrace to the other, and I didn't think I took one step on my own.

Maybe I even blacked out for a while. When I could breathe again I discovered I had a plate in one hand, a drink in the other, and a fellow I knew back in New York was standing next to me talking a mile a minute.

Back in New York this fellow had been a quiet businessman, always in the dark double-breasted suit, the conservative tie, the well-tailored overcoat. I could not get over what had happened to him.

"This is not the way you used to dress, Roger," I told him.

"This is what they all wear here," he answered, not even blushing.

"This" was as close as you could come to nothing and still have something. Roger was wearing shorts—not long shorts but short shorts—a white shirt opened to the waist and turned back so you could get a better view of his chest. To keep off colds, a bandana was knotted around his throat. Apart from a pair of sandals that was it. And Roger was not a young man, nor could he have doubled in physique for the local lifeguard.

Still he was in the swim. Every man had on a similar outfit. Some had on even less. The women were wearing strapless sun dresses or halters and shorts, or shorts and scarves tied around their tops. All you saw, east and west, was human flesh. I was glad you ate hors d'oeuvres with your fingers. I would have been scared to use a fork. One false move and I would have drawn blood.

"People ought to be leaving soon," I said to Roger.

"Oh, no," he told me, "they don't leave for hours. Not hours. And when this batch leaves, more will be coming. Look."

I looked. The mob waiting had doubled. They were walking up each other's backs.

"You would never have got inside," Roger said, "if one of the strongest men on the Riviera hadn't been behind you pushing."

We talked a little more between moments of being elbowed, and Roger told me it would be eleven o'clock before the place got human again.

"They don't even stop to eat dinner," he said.

Since we were old friends I told him frankly that I wanted to meet some people, and did he have any suggestions? I could see people meeting each other and arranging to go out all around me, but I figured that there should be an easier way. I told Roger there *must* be an easier way as the last hors d'oeuvres got knocked off my plate.

He wasn't sure it was any easier, but Roger said there was the place where everybody went swimming—Eden Roc. It was a half hour's drive from Cannes, and he offered to take me there in his car the following morning. I said I would be delighted, thinking it was far better to be launched from his Ford than from Sybella's runabout. I thanked him, let two fat women kick and shove me to the door, and had dinner in my room.

Bright and early the next morning at eleven o'clock I was ready: black bathing suit, dark glasses, beach bag full of paraphernalia, and an eager, shining face. I had been told "Roc," so I suppose I should have guessed. I don't know what I expected, but a strip of sand at least was somewhere in my mental picture. There isn't a grain of sand within miles of Eden Roc. It was merely

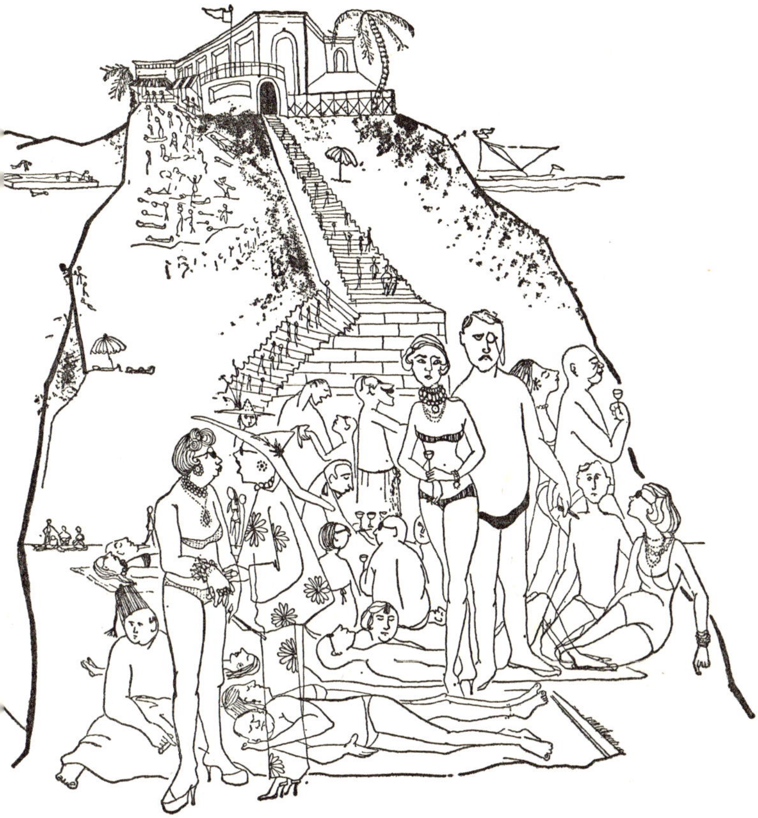

a pile of rocks and cement that tumbled down into the water. You couldn't even see the rocks and cement right off, it was so covered with people. They were sitting and lying in every nook, cranny, and corner. In fact, Eden Roc looks exactly like a gathering spot for penguins, a kind of penguin Harvest Home. I got a bath towel and started to shop around for a foot or so of vacant space. If you've ever been in a cafeteria with a loaded tray and no table to sit at, you'll know how I felt. Besides, if I had been underdressed at the gala, I felt sure overdressed on the Roc. The Bikinis Junie had talked about were tents compared to what the sun bathers were sporting. The women wore two threads that had been woven for them by a world-famous *couturier*, who had probably hired some world-famous spiders for the job; the men had their bathing suits rolled down to the gasping point. If anyone there had taken a deep breath the last shreds of decency would have been down the drain. From the stares, I gathered none of the crowd had seen a one-piece bathing suit since Grandfather stopped cranking the Model T. At last I found an empty corner and curled up in it, trying to be as small and inconspicuous as possible, plus doing a little hitching up of my bathing suit at the bottom and a little tucking down at the top.

Roger had already skipped away somewhere. Probably he couldn't stand being seen in the company of someone who was wearing the kind of bathing suit I was. It was the first time I had heard of a man being embarrassed because a girl had too many clothes on.

When I had pulled myself together enough to look

around, about four mostly naked bodies down, I recognized a fugitive from Hollywood, a former actor who had been living in Europe for the past five or six years. We caught each other's eye half a dozen times; finally he pulled off his dark glasses, came over, sat down, and complained. He had one big complaint: Americans. Americans, the uncouth things, he said, were simply *overrunning* Europe, overrunning it and ruining it. The vulgarians. Why, they were forcing up prices and destroying simplicity all over the place, and weren't their manners awful, and they certainly didn't have any culture, and as far as knowing how to dress, it wasn't worth discussing.

"Well, Shaw," I said to him (that was his name—Shaw), "I don't think it's all that bad. And after all I'm an American myself, and so are you."

He seemed to get mad at this crude remark. He looked away from me and took the opportunity to exchange greetings with two French people, a German, and a British couple. He also gave three of his countrymen stares that hung icicles off their ears, even though it was a hot sunny day. I found that there are lots of Americans like Shaw. They will befriend Egyptians, be buddies with Hungarians, give the glad hello to Italians, Spaniards, any race at all, so long as it isn't American. Why this is I don't know. Maybe it makes them feel big, as if they had discovered Europe all by themselves and were going to keep it that way.

Talking with these foreigners made Shaw brighten up a lot. He turned back to me and said, "You and I are Americans, all right, but we're *different*." He didn't say in what way, but he was satisfied with his own answer. I let him be. I didn't want to get into an argument, and besides, he kept introducing me to all his friends. Before you could say, "Esperanto," we were chattering in our broken languages, and I had three invitations to dinner, six for cocktails, and a lot of others for what I guessed was lunch. It's always hard for me to remember what the word for lunch is in foreign languages.

The invitations came in the nick of time too, because there was a bright flash above us, a "Hello, darleeng," and Sybella was in the act again. She was wearing a pair of sunburst pajamas like in a thirties movie (even Sybella didn't have the gall to put that figure into a Bikini), and she had another tired businessman in tow. He was forgetting his cares and worries with her, and he was also forgetting how to balance his checkbook. She swept down toward us, around bodies, pausing to find out who everyone was, how much money they had, who was getting it. You could say she was doing her daily dozen—collecting information for the day.

Shaw was green under his tan.

"You don't like her either?" I asked him. It developed that when he had come to Europe years ago, Sybella had made a considerable dent in his savings. Much as he hated to breathe a word against a European, however low, he had to admit that he would gladly see Sybella frying in butter.

There was no escape though. Down she came, bawling me out for not having phoned her. "Seely child, what do you theenk you are doing? You cannot just seet around heere with these people. Am I not right, Shaw, darleeng?" Shaw just mumbled to himself. "Come along weeth me, Dorees," she said. "We weel have lunch together." Trapped again. There was nothing for me to do but say yes.

By way of saying good-by to Shaw and his friends, she shrugged her shoulders. Then she ran up the Roc like a ring-tailed monkey, her diamonds flashing in the sun, with Tired Charley and me trudging along behind.

I gathered from Sybella, and the number of people around, that the restaurant at Eden Roc was a very chic place. During my stay at Cannes I grew to like it. They had awfully good fresh strawberry juice there—awfully good with a split of Pol Roger poured in it, I mean. Still, like every place, the dining room had its little hazard. It was a financial one. It was not quite safe to eat there, especially by yourself. Sometimes you would find yourself sitting alone in the middle of your demitasse, after being surrounded by a dozen gay pals at luncheon. They had all felt a crying need of a dip in the sea, or they had left their priceless cameras in a precarious spot, or they just had to fix their pompadours. And you were left with *l'addition,* which I found out fast is French for the check. One wealthy girl came to Cannes knowing only one French phrase, *"S'il vous plait, donnez-moi l'addition."* She was pointed out as the smartest hostess at Eden Roc.

Another wealthy American, when asked why he slept so late in the morning, was heard to say it was because he had to rest his arm, it got sore from picking up all those checks.

Anyway, that first day in the Eden Roc restaurant

Sybella really passed out introductions over our hot and cold hors d'oeuvres. Her friends (they were the same ones, I guess, that had been too good for me) seemed so happy to meet me. In the beginning I thought they were merely being cordial. As time went by, and I got to know the Roc better, I found out the hard way that they had taken a leaf from Sybella. By the hard way, I mean I got stuck for three big luncheon checks before I realized I was with experts. Sybella's friends were to sticking people with checks what Culbertson was to bridge.

Some of them were franker than the rest. They didn't come up to your table as if they had intentions of paying. They openly hung around waiting for lunch invitations. There was one French playboy who used to leave the Roc at noon, climb to the top, and look down at everyone still lying in the sun. He was waiting for someone to ask him to have something to eat with them. He looked like nothing so much as a hungry eagle ready to swoop down on its prey. He usually succeeded in finding a host, but once in a while his luck ran out, and he was found later drinking beer in the bar and eating the free chips, glumly thinking over his doom.

Getting free meals wasn't their only dodge. I sometimes got bored just sitting, shimmering in the sun all day long. So when one of Sybella's friends suggested a game of gin rummy, I was glad to play with him. Until he added up the score and told me what I owed him. It sounded like an awful lot of francs, but I paid him, thinking of honorable debts and how you should always pay them. Later I told Shaw about it.

"Doris," he said, "don't ever play gin rummy or canasta or any kind of cards with those boy playmates of Sybella's. You will be out thousands of francs if you do. Those boys keep score with a spoon."

Those weren't the only kind of people Sybella knew. They were the only kind she would introduce me to though. She kept her favorite type to herself. When it came time to introduce *him*, she would get a sudden fit of coughing, or be involved in conversation, or plain forget my name. Her favorite type, of course, was an American just the opposite of Shaw. He was glad to see anyone, anyone at all; he paid, paid, paid, night and day, for the privilege of being a member of a group. It made no difference if the group was Greek or strictly from St. Louis. He would hop around the Roc, being sociable with everything on it, people, waiters, attendants, seaweed, snails, anything. I guess the only reason he didn't have a flock of twenty dollar bills pinned to his bathing suit was because his bathing suit was too small. The weight of the money he used every day would have dragged it all out of shape. Still, he enjoyed himself, and he could afford it, so why not, is what I say. Not that I got much of anything out of it. Sybella would let him wander to the extent of a few lunches, or maybe even a dinner, but when it came to large parties, or money for gambling, or anything big, it was better to get out of her way, quick, at those times. To have been in her way would have been like standing in the path of an enraged threshing machine.

At least my début on Eden Roc wasn't like my experience at the gala. I had met Shaw's friends, and

Sybella's, and I saw a lot of my own friends, the ones I had heard talking about Europe in those bistros back in New York. They were having as big a time as they said they were going to, spending money, getting some laughs, and just loving being back in Europe, darling.

In a week, I looked and acted like the rest of the people who went to Eden Roc. I bought myself a conservative Bikini, developed a tan, went up and down the Roc saying "Hello," and talking to people. I could dodge the chiselers, I knew pretty much who was chic or at least solvent. I ate my lunch, which was quite a business, flopped into the icy water from the ladders, and waited for someone to pull me out again (which is the only way you could get out, once you were in), just like the old hands.

And in the process, I met millionaires all right. It wasn't too easy, because you could hardly tell a millionaire from a bum, around there, the clothes everyone wore. They never got out of those wispy cotton dresses, turned-back skirts, bandanas, and shorts. (A popular joke was: "Ah, it's you! I didn't recognize you with your clothes on.") You could tell at a glance though, that it was the women at Cannes who were really rolling in money. They furnished you with a clue to their financial standing. Jewels. One American woman would sit around sipping her iced drinks in a calico dress that must have set her back all of four dollars and ninety-five cents. On her wrists, fingers, and around her neck was half a million dollars worth of jewelry. There wasn't a zircon in the carload. (There were lots of women who had zircon jewelry, and they never took it off either.)

With shorts, bathing suits, tennis dresses, it was diamonds and emeralds all the way. You can be sure that the young men I had noticed at the gala never left the side of those jewels.

When you did find out from a reliable source that a man was a millionaire in spite of the few rags he was wearing, if you heard he was also an American millionaire, you dropped the whole thing then and there. It was a sure thing some Sybella had snared him before he had walked two steps off the boat gangplank.

If he was a European millionaire, you still had trouble. The trouble was the rate of exchange. Change a French millionaire, for instance, from francs to dollars, and he's demoted to a commuter, struggling to meet the mortgage. With European millionaires, it's not a question of how rich he is, but how well you like a certain country. A European millionaire is only good in his own country, which is an important thing for every girl to remember.

The difficulties with millionaires caused me to complain some. However, I could not complain that there was any lack of amusement. Life was gay and grand; there were dinner parties, lunches, gambling, and yacht parties.

I get a thrill out of yacht parties. The boats look so white and pretty on the water, and it's dashing to be called for by a launch and go churning on to your cocktails and dinner. As much as I liked them, I cannot say I had luck with the yacht parties I went to. One time, for example, we had been out cruising around the whole day, and were heading back to Cannes in the late afternoon. There was quite a large group of us, and all the other girls were French. The party had been fun and nothing especial happened, until I decided to spend the last hours of the trip taking a sun bath. I found that the other girls had the same idea, only there they were lying nonchalantly in full view of the men, and every one of them had taken off the top half of her bathing suit. I dived below like a rabbit and spent the remaining two hours combing my hair. It's a wonder it didn't all fall out.

Then there was the time the movie star was the guest of honor at a yacht party. I am pretty hardened to movie stars; my experience has led me to take them or leave them, but this star was an exception. Fergus, I'll call him, was the all-time European film muscleman. When he came leaping into Technicolor scenes, the hair on his chest in full view, cities fell, villains got stabbed with swords, women were carried off making no objection. And here I was, seated next to him on a lovely yacht, the Mediterranean moonlight in full glow. I thought, "If he tried to kiss me, I certainly would not set up a howl." Leaning closer, I asked him how things were going at his country home, which I knew he had. His eyes lit up with a fervent light, he turned to me, all enthusiasm. "It's wonderful," he said, "and you should just see the garden this year. Why the Canterbury bells alone would make it a perfectly beautiful thing." So I rolled up my *décolletage* five notches, and passed the evening agreeing with him that larkspur was one of the most attractive blossoms in all this world.

It was the dancing yacht party that made the biggest

impression on me though. This was an afternoon affair, complete with champagne, distinguished guests, and an orchestra playing away, up on the very top part of the yacht, whatever they call it. I was having a sensational time and so were the other dancers, when we heard a commotion. We looked out, and there was an enormous Italian liner bearing right down on us. I don't know today if the liner was somewhere it shouldn't have been, or whether the captain of the yacht had been sneaking rather too much champagne. Whichever way it was, it was a close call. The captain slewed the yacht around at a ninety-degree angle, and we missed the liner. No one was hurt, but the entire orchestra, which was still playing along way up in the air, didn't expect the turn, and every man in it slid right off the deck into the water. They were fishing piccolo players and drummers out of the Mediterranean for days.

Yacht owners had another little habit that led to some misunderstanding. They would invite people out, have the party; in the middle of it they would get an inspiration, and the next thing you knew, you were sailing along the coast of North Africa, on a delightful impromptu cruise. Delightful if you didn't care what happened on shore, that is, and most people kind of did care what was happening on shore. This never happened to me; I did know a couple of girls whose lives were practically ruined by unexpected cruises. A beau doesn't mind waiting a few hours, but when hours run into weeks, he is liable to become unhappy.

Dinner parties on land were generally fun and not as loaded with trouble. Even here there were exceptions.

A Cannes dinner party—one that Shaw, the American American-hater, gave—is an example. We were seated around in a nice restaurant, eating good French food. There were three other girls along, one very vivacious, who was known for being an expert at shuffling and re-dealing her men friends. This night she was with an American I knew, Bob, and they were laughing and having themselves a big evening. Bob was across the table from me and I noticed over his shoulder a man at the next table looking awfully mad and gloomy. This went on until dessert. I looked up again, and shouted, "That man has a knife!" Had it not been for a waiter who caught his arm, the gloomy man would have made Bob about as alive as a plate of spare ribs. I do not need to say the would-be knifer was a soul who had been put into the discard pack by the vivacious girl. Feelings run high on the Riviera.

I went to the parties and the dinners and the lunches, and I met more and more millionaires. Egyptian millionaires, English millionaires, French millionaires. But none of them suited me. I didn't want to settle in Egypt; I had heard the climate was awful in England, and though I thought France was wonderful, I couldn't see myself staying there for life. After all, I am still a patriotic American, and never pretended to be anything else.

Still, I repeat that Cannes was fun, once you got the hang of it. It is strictly a "give a little, take a little, and duck fast" setup, but truly glamorous in its way. If only it had contained the millionaire that was missing in my life.

Just when I began to think I had come all the way to Europe merely to wind up looking for an American in the crowd, Fate, who had not been looking my way, gave me a glance. And in a way I had never expected at all. It happened an evening after I had been in Cannes about a month or so, and this evening was the first time I had ever gambled there. I know what I can do, and what I don't know how to do. I had never gambled, realized I didn't understand it, and wouldn't have gone near the casino if it hadn't been for The Drum.

Now The Drum is about the only night spot in Cannes that has dancing. Restaurants Cannes has, good ones; places to gamble, but not dancing except at The Drum. In The Drum all the customers are tight as one; it is in the old section of Cannes, and it is without a doubt the dirtiest, darkest, loosest night club in the world. Also the patrons who are crammed into this trap represent as much money per dark, filthy inch as you will find in any night club in the world. To get in the door you have to cross an alley that looks as if it ought to have a sign hanging on it that reads, "Pepe le Moko was here." Persistent whispers had it that if an unescorted girl tried to cross it she would be knocked senseless and carried off by white slavers. I often thought, what's the difference? Unescorted or with twelve men surrounding you, a girl was knocked senseless anyway by the unholy blast of music from what was carelessly called an orchestra. Or, once inside, there was a ninety-to-ten chance of getting pushed galley west by an inebriated patron's elbow as he was in the process of demonstrating an uninhibited jungle dance. Many was the evening in The Drum, as I sat looking at some guy wearing a gold pirate earring fall flat on his face as he pawed after a girl, or some woman clawing another woman's hair out, that I wished those old white slavers would come along and take the place over. Compared to the regular customers, they would have been as tame as a covey of earnest divinity students.

But The Drum was the only place in Cannes where you could dance. That was the big excuse, and like the rest of the people in Cannes I got dragged there night after night.

This night it was especially awful, and I was about ready to stand up and scream, which would have been a waste of time the noise was so terrible, when the White Russian I was with suggested going over to the casino and having some gambling. I would have leaped at a chance to go to the pits and have boiling oil poured over me. In no time at all we were driving up in front of the casino.

Outside, a Riviera gambling casino looks like a cross between a Moorish opera house and Sister Aimee Semple McPherson's Gospel Temple. Inside, it looks the same only more so. Except for the tables and the players, who certainly don't resemble people who go to the opera or go to church. The casinos never close, are open twenty-four hours a day. The air is dead white, a mass of smoke that doesn't even move. Around the important tables, you notice the girls again, the International Vultures, or Sybella Set. They sit there like rows of Mata Haris, covered of course with jewels, which they show off by crossing their hands over each other in fancy ways when they pick up cards or chips. (Perhaps this is to prevent one hand from knowing what the other is doing.) Taking cigarettes or chips out of boxes studded with precious stones, they really know what they are doing, don't miss a play, and usually come out well ahead.

My Russian wandered off, leaving me with some bundles of francs. Not knowing what to do at all, I tried the roulette table. You have heard of a one-armed bandit. Well, roulette is a two-armed monster, there are no other words for it. What scared me most was that I had won quite a lot, and hadn't the smallest idea how I'd done it. So I quickly collected my winnings and went on to another impressive-looking table.

Out of the frying pan into the fire was a joke alongside of what I had done. I was playing *chemin de fer*. Now you will rarely see Americans playing *chemin de fer*. There is a good reason for this. *Chemin de fer* didn't get its name—the railroad—for nothing. It's faster than a berserk express. Minutes don't count, it's that golden thirtieth of a second. If you don't open your mouth then, you're out five thousand francs. The game is all conducted in French, naturally, and you've got to know French cold to play it; not just know French pretty well, or all right, but *cold*. That's why Americans stay away from it as a rule. Besides, I don't think that Americans are used to that kind of gambling, and *chemin de fer* is as simple as the wiring system on a subway. If you think it's sitting at a table in a sweat shirt and saying, "Craps," you couldn't be more wrong.

The game is a rat race, and there is a language trap; and that isn't all. Oh, no! Not only are people betting on the game; people are betting on the people who are betting on the game. That's how the Sybellas win mostly. They watch and see who's winning; if he's skillful and seems to be lucky they start putting money on him. It's all in the game. Then there is the silent language—nods, winks, and gestures. They can mean I'll take half your bet, or I'll bank you, or we'll go out tonight. I sure couldn't tell you what it all signified.

I was just stuck on this awful train. I never knew if I'd won or lost except when the scoop came along. If my money was still there, I'd leave it alone; if some was taken away, I'd put more down. When I found out later what I could have done, I still get the chills. Why, a European man who had been playing *chemin de fer* for years forgot himself a second, said *Banco* instead of *Carte,* and lost two million francs before the word was half out of his mouth.

Furthermore, in my confusion I had nearly crossed up the game completely. I had ordered a drink (I never needed one so much in my life) and set it on the table next to my purse and gloves. At this a hush fell over the crowd; men snarled, women sneered. A phalanx of waiters tore over, snatched the glass off the gaming table, and put it in back of my chair on a special little table. That's the one thing that will stop a game of *chemin de fer.* It's a law like something engraved on a stone tablet; never set a drink on a gaming table, always on the little table in back of you.

Never did I think I would wish I was back in The

Drum, no matter how tough things got. At that moment I wished I was back in The Drum. Not knowing if I was ahead or behind, or how or when I could stop playing, I looked around wildly for the Russian. He was so deep in a roulette game that he wouldn't have seen anything but black and red if the place had been on fire.

It was just at this point when a voice behind me asked, "Eet ees zat you have trouble, senorita?"

I said, "Get me out of this thing."

In a second or two I was away from the table clutching my money. Even if the man who had rescued me had been pure Neanderthal, he would have been a hero to me. But he wasn't—not at all. In gratitude I told him that I must buy him a glass of champagne. He said he would be glad to have one if I would permit him to buy it. I was unwilling, but I finally agreed. So we sat and drank a glass of champagne while I counted my money. By a miracle I was still a winner—not by much, to be sure, but a winner. One of the most dazed winners the casino had ever seen.

As the mist began to lift, I turned my attention to José-Armada. He was most attractive, in fact, and very sympathetic. Somehow I trusted him on sight and told him all my woes. He was so nice and asked if he could call me at my hotel the next day. I said yes, and he did.

We sat on the Roc and talked about America, which he had visited. We had lunch and talked about people in general. We had dinner and talked about people we knew in particular. We went out constantly—dancing, on yachts, swimming. It was wonderful. The blank had been filled; there was an interesting man in my life, and he was a millionaire. He was Spanish, and remembering what I found out about the rate of exchange, I asked him what the country was like. I have never heard anyone go on like that; he was absolutely wild about the place. He said I would love it, adore it, that I must go there. He convinced me. I made up my mind to go to Spain.

José-Armada was going to Tangiers on business; he would be back in Spain within three weeks and show me his country. In the meantime he would cable a friend of his to meet me, who would take me around, introduce me to people while José-Armada was in Tangiers.

Cannes was as gay as ever, but I had had enough of yachts, gambling, The Drum, and jockeying around the lunch table. I flew back to Paris to get a few clothes and in a matter of days was on a Spanish plane bound for Madrid.

Sybella had warned me against going there, back in Cannes. "Darleeng," she had said, tipping her mauve-brown-chartreuse-and-navy striped sun hat to one side, "you weel not like eet there. No, you are fooleesh going. You weel not like the people there."

"Do you know them?" I asked her.

"Oh, yes, but of course I know them, and you weel not like them."

If she didn't like them, I figured I'd get along fine. Remembering what she had said only made me wish the plane would get to Madrid faster.

CHAPTER 7

I ALMOST BECOME
A BULLFIGHTER

WHEREVER THERE ARE SPANIARDS, THEY make a little bit of Spain. You could tell it right away, on this Spanish plane. It was so different from the one I had crossed the Atlantic on. There were no assigned seats, no lists of the other passengers' names, but while the plane was still tilted in the air, taking off, everybody was already in the aisles, talking, laughing, and finding out who everybody else was. Spain is small, people are interested in what is going on; in Spain everyone really knows everybody else's business. As far as getting the local news and passing it around, Spain has any small town in America beaten hollow.

Then there were no "Please Fasten Your Safety Belt" or "No Smoking" signs on the plane. I wondered about this; after I had been in Spain awhile I didn't wonder any more. You cannot tell a Spaniard what to do, you simply can't. It's impossible. Why, there was one street corner in Madrid—every day somebody got run over crossing it. This went on until the police decided it had to stop. So they set up a series of metal markers to show people which way to go safely, and stationed some of their men on the corner to see that people actually walked between the markers. In no time at all, there were mobs collected on that corner, and when a man would make a break and run across the old way, the crowd would cheer him. It was a new sport, almost like bullfighting, to see if he'd get across. The police had to give up after a week of struggle. You cannot tell a Spaniard what to do. If he doesn't have a dime, and you give him some money and try to give him some advice at the same time, he will throw the money down, spit in your eye, and walk away. Spaniards are proud. Threaten one and you've had it.

I wanted to get to my hotel quick, as José-Armada had told his good friend Juan to meet me and take me to dinner that very evening. When the plane landed (the way we were tipping sidewise and dropping I had my doubts that it ever would land—Spanish pilots must think you are paying for thrills, not simply boring transportation), there was a whole barricade of people at the airport, all of them gaping at me. I guess it was because I looked so different from Spanish girls. Reporters were taking my picture like crazy, figuring no doubt that a girl who was tall and blonde would sooner or later make her mark in Spain. They were not wrong.

It was rough going, getting into Madrid. The taxicab that took me made the ones in Paris look like a fleet of

1960 Cadillacs. The taxi was cracked, mended, wheezing, and lopsided. And old! It was absolutely square and you sat up so high you thought you were in a Mack truck. Not to mention the donkeys. The streets were just loaded with donkeys, pulling wooden carts. Those donkeys were as old and grisly as the taxi, and it was a fight to the death between them.

Anyway, we pulled up to the Hotel Velásquez without any casualties on either side. Though I liked the Hotel Velásquez, I didn't stay there long. I couldn't pronounce it just right, and the Spanish taxi drivers wouldn't take a try at understanding my American accent. A taxi driver would just sit there with his hands folded on the wheel, until I could get a Spanish friend to pronounce it right for him. Then his face would break out in smiles, and we'd shoot off, lurching from side to side, our fenders banging into donkeys and people crossing the wrong way. If I hadn't shown the driver a piece of paper on which José-Armada had written it down, I would never have gotten to the Hotel Velásquez in the first place. By the time I had learned to pronounce it right, I had moved to the Palace Hotel.

When I got settled in my room in the Velásquez, I sat and tried to decide when to dress. I decided I would wait until Juan telephoned me. The hours went by; it got to be seven o'clock, then eight. The first thing I thought of was the telephone. Maybe it was like the Paris telephone, and Juan had been trying to get me, and had been getting fish markets, barbershops, and three other girls instead.

I found a maid who spoke a little English, and she

explained to me that the phone worked, all right. And what was more, you could make all the local calls you wanted to for free! I was thrilled, and my whole time in Spain, I talked on the telephone half the day every day. Everyone did. Mothers called children, wives yakked with friends, men were cackling over a new conquest, and the girls were giving each other the lowdown. If there is one thing a girl likes to do, it is to call up a girl friend and tell her what happened the night before; what he said, how he looked, where they went, if they had a fight, and all the rest. So Spain was a girl's paradise. They can tell all absolutely without cost.

That still didn't tell me what had happened to Juan. Maybe he hadn't gotten the cable. Maybe he had the wrong day. (Like any other woman, I would not even hint to myself that there was a possibility I had been stood up.) I told myself I was tired from the plane ride, and tumbled into bed, mad as a hornet. At nine thirty, the phone rang. It was Juan, saying he would call for me around ten thirty for cocktails, if I could be ready then. "Cocktails at ten thirty!" I thought. "He must be out of his Iberian head." I was too mad to sleep anyhow, so we agreed to have him call for me at ten thirty.

We went to the smaller of the two night clubs that are the chic of Madrid. I had thought that Maxim's in Paris drew a mixed group of customers; this Spanish spot made it seem like a storm cellar for charter members of the Union Club. In no time at all, I saw what the system was. It was not that you were social, not that you were attractive, it was the fact you got there first. Clerks were grinning away at tables right on top of the dance floor, while *duques* had to stumble out of their cobwebby corners over fifty pairs of feet before they and their partners could sneak in a fox trot or two. The clerks had arrived first; it was first come, first served and seated, and no holds barred.

I also saw that everyone around was having cocktails too, so I figured that Juan had not been pulling a dodge for being lazy about appointments. We finished our cocktails around eleven thirty, had our dinner over by twelve thirty. At first we looked at each other kind of askance, the way friends of friends always do. Pretty soon I thawed out; Juan looked like the Spaniard of storybook and song, dark, romantic, full of temperament. And he was tall for a Spaniard, which was a good thing. As far as I could tell, he had taken a liking to me too. The trouble was, we had a language barrier. He could not speak English; he could understand it though, if spoken slowly. My conversational French was *pas bon,* but I could understand it all right. So I would talk to him in English, and he would answer me in French. It was bad in one way; in another, it was a good thing. All the time Juan and I knew each other we never had a fight. We couldn't—we didn't have words enough.

Just as we were really going great guns, they announced the club was closing for the evening. It was two in the morning, but on the Spanish schedule of things, it was only the beginning. All that was left open in Madrid were the grubby dives, the local color places. Juan asked me if I minded going to one, and I was feeling so gay and happy that I said, "Not at all." This dump was situated in a network of alleys. If I had been accidentally separated from Juan it would have been good-by, or *adios,* to use the native expression. Like dumps the world over, this one was raucous, smoky, unclean, filled with what I was forced to call characters, because to use any other word for them would not have been ladylike. There was one unique feature though. I looked around at all the bad dancers and character girls, and said, surprised, "Why Juan, not a single one of these girls is wearing a stitch of underwear beneath those ghastly satin dresses." He only laughed. My hunch is maybe underwear is terribly scarce in Spain.

In spite of the underwear shortage, it was an awfully pleasant evening, and I hoped I would see Juan again. After a few days I was sure he had really warmed up to me. He called, sent me big baskets of flowers. We went driving, we went to polo matches and night clubs. And he was going to give a party for me, to present me to his friends. It seemed to be the only way to meet people in Spain. There was the Palace Bar, which was almost as much of a central spot as the Carlton Terrace had been on the Riviera. But even if you were the most beautiful girl in the world, you could sit in the Palace Bar day after day, and few Spaniards would even look at you. You would begin to think you had been looking in trick mirrors all those years. In Spain, you have got to be introduced at a party.

I had only been in Spain about a week, and as always, half my luggage was still on the way. I did have one terrific dress from Paris I planned to wear to my party, or début. It was black, street length, thin-skirted, with big panels floating out on either side. The afternoon of the party, I sent it out to the hotel valet to be pressed. When I got back from an early dinner, there it was, lying neatly on my bed. It looked wonderful on the bed. On me it looked just a little peculiar. In pressing it, they had stretched the skirt till it bagged around my ankles like the trousers Wallace Beery used to wear in pictures, and after all, there was no getting away from it, the gown *had* been designed to be street length, and wasn't meant to be worn in bed.

I rang for the maid and asked her for a needle and thread, thinking I could shorten it. That way it might not be just as the *couturier* imagined it, but on the other hand, no one would think I was selling apples. The maid was horrified. Didn't the senorita know that one could not get needle and thread except on the black market? And that the black market wasn't open this time of night? So there I was, feeling like the man who has left his money in his other suit. Only in my case, it was the girl who had left her needle, thread, and other dresses in her other suitcase.

In desperation, I stalked around my rooms, thinking what to do. I spotted a bundle of papers, my passport and so on, and they were held together by a rubber band. Being careful not to stretch it to the breaking point, I slipped the rubber band around my waist, and hiked up the extra yards of skirt over it. The side panels came in handier than I had ever dreamed they would, because they hid the worst billows. So I sallied out, looking, if plumper than usual, at least quite chic. The only thing was, of course I couldn't walk when I got there, or the skirt would slip down. I would have to spend all my party sitting down.

Juan's car and chauffeur were waiting for me. Riding over to his house, I tried to think about books on deportment, and if they had anything to say about sitting down during a whole party when you didn't have any obvious reason for it, like a broken leg or being pregnant. Then I remember one line that went: "Choose a chair in front of the fireplace, sit straight in it, and you will command the room." I didn't particularly want to command the room, I only didn't want my dress to disgrace me—but if I could prevent that and command the room all in one blow, why, that was fine with me.

Madrid houses are like New York town houses, thin and tall. As I climbed the stairs to the drawing room, past tapestries, coats of armor, and dim oil paintings, I prayed that it would have a fireplace. I could barely greet Juan politely, because there it was! Not just a little fireplace, but one you could have driven a Buick around in comfortably, all carved marble, with a mantel that would have been above my head if I had stood under it. I didn't; I sat down in the great high-backed armchair in front of it so fast several people thought I had dropped through a hole in the floor. And I stayed put, right in that chair, the entire evening, only moving to take a cigarette from my case, and to hitch up my skirt over the rubber band when I hoped no one was looking. I don't know if I can recommend the advice the book gave—since it was my party, everyone had to come over to me anyway, so I suppose I did command the room. Perhaps it wouldn't work in every situation, and I myself never tried it again.

At Juan's party, sitting still was the best thing I could have done. Until they get to know you, Spanish women act toward an American girl like a bunch of mean dogs. You can't talk to them first, you've got to wait until they come and talk to you. That way they'll think a lot more of you. In the meantime, talk to the men. They'll think a lot more of you too. I will add, that once you get to know them, Spanish women are awfully sweet; kind, polite, and loyal. And patient! The murder those Spanish men get away with, without their wives or sweethearts making so much as a complaint, would cause an American middle-aged businessman to writhe—with envy. That night, they hadn't gotten to know me, and I could hear their remarks, delivered mostly in French, which they knew I understood. It was my blonde hair, and wasn't I awfully old, and though the rest of my figure seemed all right, didn't I have an awful bulge around my middle? I longed to tell them that the bulge was strictly Dior overlap; instead I decided to wait and bide my time.

The men were charming. They fetched me wine, lit my cigarettes, talked to me in different broken languages. They didn't seem to mind my bulge, and rubber band or no rubber band, I was what you could call a hit.

All the men there seemed to have titles, which threw me for a loss. They had so many, two or three apiece; one for day in and day out, and a couple to spare. One man would be Pepe. Fine; his cronies called him Pepe. I called him Pepe. He was also Pepe, Duque de Situacion. Great; I knew that too. Where I fell down was with the spare titles, because he was Pepe, Duque de Situacion y Marques de Suburb y Conde de Who Knows. Those I couldn't straighten out. Usually, there were a couple of Spanish nicknames thrown in, just to brighten things up. During the whole party I never knew when Pepe was a *duque,* when he was a *marques,* or when he was the Spanish equivalent of old Bitsy. All evening I kept claiming I didn't know someone; I would be introduced and I would find out it was friend Pepe again, bobbing up under another set of names.

They were awfully good natured about it, and as I say, I was quite a hit. So as a special thing, Juan and his friends invited me to watch flamenco dancing the next night, and to attend a flamenco feast. They picked me up at my hotel, a group of us went out to dinner, and went dancing until the clubs closed at two. Considering that dinner isn't over until one o'clock, this is as unfair and frustrating as if New York night clubs closed at ten.

Anyway, Juan said to me, "Now we weel go to the Jardin Verde, and I weel make a flamenco for you." I couldn't wait.

We headed for the Jardin Verde. I don't know what was in my mind—a garden at least, with a semi-palace rising in the middle of it. But it looked like it should have been in an alley instead of twenty minutes out of Madrid in the countryside. One of the men told me it had formerly been a brothel years ago, and inexperienced in these matters as I am, I had it spotted for just that. Inside it looked exactly like any brothel in a stage-set. It was hard enough to get inside—you had to take your life in your hands, and drive up the narrowest curbed driveway in Spain, which is to say in the universe.

I was told a funny story about it. A *marques*, a friend of Juan's, would go every night to the Jardin Verde for drinks with his friends after the clubs closed in town. Every night he would drive his long, low, beautiful car into the stone-walled, spaghetti-thin driveway, and every night he would dent or scratch the fenders. He got so mad that he traded in his big car for a little one. He took it all perfectly seriously and said to me when I asked him about it, "Why, Miss Leely, eet was an een-convenience, theese bumped fenders, no?"

Things, as we say in America, were jumping at the Jardin Verde. More girls with no underwear, more drunks, more smoke, more yelling. And the music, such a razzmatazz as I have never heard. "Is this flamenco," I thought, "the famous folk music of Spain? If so, Dizzie Gillespie is Mozart."

I sat there in silence, which wasn't hard, since I couldn't express my feelings anyway, so disappointed the tears almost came to my eyes. In about an hour, Juan took my hand and said, "You weel come upstairs now, yes?"

"The last straw," I thought, "the very last. He may call it flamenco, but at home it's known as the old one-four." Fortunately while I was still struggling to say something dignified but firm, I saw, out of the corner of my eye, the rest of the party all climbing the stairs. Unless this is an orgy, which I strongly doubt, it may yet turn out to be flamenco, I reflected, and went upstairs with Juan.

The room on the second floor was very different from the one downstairs; elegant, quiet, no one in it but our group. On one side of it there were enough chairs and sofas for all of us. The rest of Juan's friends sat down; I did too. Across the room there was another, smaller arrangement of chairs; in a few minutes, five people came in and sat in them. They were gypsies all right, and very young, with wild, big eyes, and long ringlets of oiled hair. Juan told me that two were guitarists, two were dancers, and one was a singer.

They started right off, singing and playing, and I knew I was really in for something. They were howling and burbling up and down the scale, the guitars were thumping away, and the dancers were stomping like crazy. It wasn't what you could call pretty, but it kind of got you after a while. It was like a tense game of canasta; you are suffering in a way, still it's too exciting to stop. About five or six in the morning, waiters came in bringing flamenco food, ham cured in the snow of the Pyrenees, and a special wine. We were all so hungry and thirsty that we ate and drank our heads off, the guests and the artists too.

Then everything went on like it had before. More singing and twanging and stomping. I even got up and stomped around with a gypsy for a while myself.

"How do you like thees, Dorees?" Juan asked me. I told him I was crazy about it. "Then you weel want to meet the Preence of the Gypsies," he said. I wasn't too sure I did. I was sure he would be some ragged, bearded old number, smelling to high heaven. The man must have stood in front of me for five minutes before I came to. The Prince of the Gypsies was as suave as either Juan or his friends, good looking with wonderful manners. I had noticed him in our party, but I hadn't had a chance to talk to him.

He explained that he was not a gypsy himself, just their kind of patron. He gave them money, looked after them, discovered and encouraged the most talented of them.

The following morning he drove me around Madrid in his car. And it was all true. Everywhere he went, there were gypsies. They would follow him down the street, calling his name. That beautiful open car was always loaded to the bumpers with gypsies getting rides here and there. If he came into a café where they were, they would shout *"Olé"* and rush over to see him. It was great fun. I got to know quite a few of them, and saw the best flamenco dancing and singing and playing anywhere in Spain.

Juan was doing his best to show me Spain, and his best was pleasing me a lot. Maybe I paid him too many compliments on his ingenuity, because he called me up one morning with something special on his mind. "Meet me at the Palace," he cried, "I have a wonderful idea!" So I did, and his idea was truly unusual. He wanted me to become the first American girl bullfighter in Spain. I would get to wear the costume, and everyone would honor me, and I would have my picture in the newspapers. Well, that appealed to me, no doubt about it.

However, though I hadn't ever seen a bullfight (the season in Madrid had not started yet), I had heard plenty about them. "Those bullfights are dangerous," I said to Juan. "I have read Hemingway, and I know. You've got to be awfully good to be a bullfighter, and even then you stand an excellent chance of winding up lying not in bed but on a slab." Juan said that the season hadn't started, so there weren't any bullfights yet, and anyhow he hadn't meant for me to actually become a bullfighter, just to get in the costume and pose in the bull ring. That I agreed to, and I saw myself looking dashing in the outfit, surrounded by reporters, and it all seemed lovely.

Juan got one of the leading bullfighters in Spain to loan me a costume. It was so effective—all that brocade, those trousers, the little hat! We drove down to the Plaza de Toros, the big bull ring of Madrid, and of Spain for that matter. It was huge, with all those empty seats, and I felt awfully small in it and kind of scared. Juan told me not to be foolish, it was only a photograph, and what could happen? So I told myself I was being foolish, and stepped out into the ring. There were swarms of reporters there, all right; they asked me all about myself, and what I did, and where I came from, and took lots and lots of pictures. "Well, that's over with, let's go back now," I said to Juan, after they seemed to have run out of questions. "Oh no," he said, "they have to take one big, authentic picture. With a

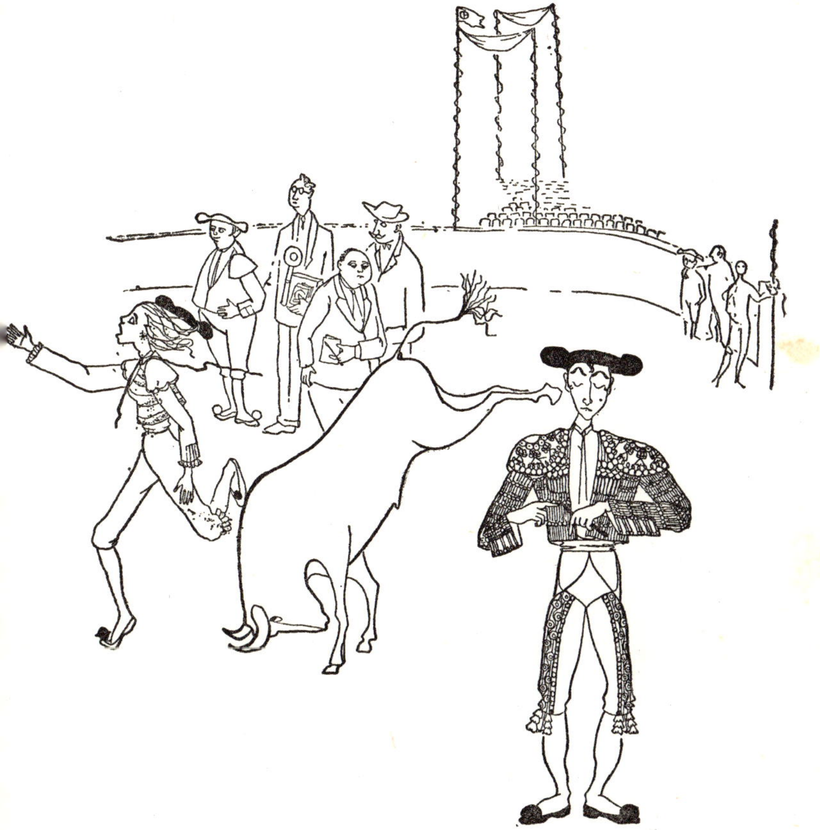

real bullfighter. Wouldn't you like to meet a real bullfighter?"

Back in America I had seen *Blood and Sand* as a movie, and I most certainly did want to meet a bullfighter. So Juan led me over to where a group of little men were standing watching, and said, "This is Ricardo, one of the greatest bullfighters in Spain."

My face must have dropped twelve feet. Ricardo looked about as much like Tyrone Power as he did like the Empire State Building. He was about two inches high, bowlegged, olive oil in his hair, and three teeth left in his mouth. His buddies and helpers, the picadors and people like that were twice as bad. It was an awful blow.

"I weel show you what to do with the *capote*," Ricardo said, with a blood-curdling smile. I thought he meant Truman Capote, but it turned out to be the bullfighters' cape he was talking about. I couldn't get half what he told me straightened out. I had to stand with my feet pointing in different directions, one hand held out in front of me, the other hand crossed over it in a special way, knees flexed, back straight, chest out, head up, and eyes rolling in confusion.

Finally he said I looked all right. There I was, my face turned to the cameras, my brocade glistening, all the ham in me out in the open, when I heard this snorting! I turned and saw a bull they had let out, tearing at me. In pictures, bulls don't look so large. Let me tell you, down in the bull ring that bull looked bigger to me than a double-decker Fifth Avenue bus. And fast! He was coming straight at me. I let out a holler, ran around in back of Ricardo, who was standing cleaning his fingernails as calm as you please, threw him the capote, and when the bull turned his attentions to him, took off out of the bull ring like a girl who would have beaten Jesse Owens in his prime.

Juan and Ricardo had the gall to try to persuade me to go back in. Needless to say, I wouldn't. Ricardo said, "He wasn't a beeg bull. Maybe he wasn't even brave." I did not feel that it was my place to challenge the bull's courage. If he was a coward, why shame him by bringing it out in the open, was my feeling. Let it be his secret.

Besides, after seeing Ricardo, the idea of bullfighters and bullfighting in general lost its charm for me. If those bullfighters all had bowlegs like Ricardo's and looked like him generally, I couldn't see how the sport had lasted as long as it had.

My picture was in all the papers, and I looked well. However, Juan sensed his idea had not been the huge success he had dreamed it would be, because I sulked for three nights and wouldn't go out with him.

We made up in the end, and went back to our polo matches, flamenco feasts, and night clubbing. Every day was fun, and like the other days. I would wake up in the morning and think, "Well, back to the tortilla mines." I loved those tortilla mines. You just got into the habit of following the pattern, and it is a fascinating pattern, you may be sure.

Madrid is the old, aristocratic city of Spain. The money, the industry, the hustling are in Barcelona; in Barcelona they work. Not in Madrid. I could set my watch by looking out of my window. When I saw Juan's car stop in front of the Palace Bar, I knew it was one in the afternoon, and that he had finished his grinding one-hour day at the office. Once I tried to tease him about it. "Don't you like to work, Juan?" I said. "Of course I like to work, Dorees," he said. "Why, I work every day of my life. Every day I am een my office at twelve sharp, and do you know I cannot go to the mountains on week ends because I must be at the office even on Saturdays?" He was genuinely hurt.

Things might have stayed placid if it had not been for one thing. José-Armada arrived on the scene. His business had kept him longer than he had expected, and he was eager to make up for lost time. He wanted to take me out that very night. I told him I would love to, but that I was going out with Juan. "Weeth Juan," he shouted, "that dirty, back-stabbing, false friend! I weel keel heem!" I soothed him a little bit, and promised to go out with him for the next four nights in a row.

I liked both Juan and José-Armada, but to tell the truth I wasn't in love with either of them at the time. They couldn't understand it. In fact, they wouldn't believe me, because in Spain it's always love—and jealousy. I never heard anyone say, "Doris and Juan went out for dinner last night," or "José-Armada and Doris are great friends." No, it's "Dorees and Juan are een love," or "José-Armada ees madly een love weeth Dorees," or "Dorees cannot decide whom she loves—Juan or José-Armada." It's love, love, love, all the time there. She left heem because she loved heem. He keeled her because he loved her. It was alarming, that's what it was.

Juan wasn't quite so much that way. He had been Americanized to some extent. For instance, he enjoyed American expressions. We were at a table in the Palace Bar one afternoon, and when he suggested leaving, I said, "Let's have one for the road." He had not heard the expression, so I told him what it meant. He was like a child, he was so delighted, and he made a game of it. "Let's have one for a side road," he would say. "Let's have one for the back road." Or, "Let's have one for the leetle path," while all his friends around the table were convulsed, and kept murmuring, "Oh, that ees so funny, Juan," and "Juan, never have you been so amusing."

Not that he wasn't jealous and violent. He would call me up at all hours of the day and night to see if I was home, and if I wasn't home, he would grill the hotel employees to find out where I was. He would go to the club, or polo match, or wherever they told him I was, take a seat or table near me and the man I was with, and mutter and glare and hiss at my escort. They seemed to expect it; so I gave up worrying and ruining my evenings over this practice.

But Juan wasn't in it with José-Armada when it came to jealousy and violence. I will give you an example of the jealousy. When I would go to the ladies' room in a Madrid restaurant or night club, José-Armada would go to the door with me. There he would make me take off my shoes, and he would keep them until I came out again. This was to prevent the possibility of me slipping out a back exit for a late date or a quick one with someone else.

As far as violence went, José-Armada's took the form of chewing. We would be sitting there, calm as you please, when I would suddenly feel this gnawing on my arm. It was José-Armada, expressing his violent love, combined with a dash of hatred (which dash is in all Spanish love). He would say to me such things as, "I weel keel you. Eet is worth years in preeson to get Dorees Leelly out of my heart." To which I would say: "What do you want to kill me for? Why get me out of your heart? I was under the impression we were having a good time." I guess he thought at moments that I wasn't romantic. This didn't make him change his ways in the slightest. Many is the evening when, in a dark corner fortunately, I thought I would lose an ear due to José-Armada's gnawing, violence, and jealousy.

The situation developed into a rivalry between José-Armada and Juan. First they stopped speaking to each other. Then they started talking about each other to their mutual friends. Then any friend of one was no friend of the other. Then they started speaking to each other again. But the things they said made my blood run cold. I began to see that this wasn't like America. It was dangerous. Something awful might happen if I didn't stop it. Something awful did happen, but not what I expected.

One afternoon I was in the Palace with José-Armada. He had gone to the bar to pay the check. I was alone, brooding over how I could cure him of his jealousy and make friends with Juan again. I heard a rattle and a laugh, and commotion and shrieks and one loud "Darleeng!" and I knew. It was none other than Sybella, her head encased in a wave of gold veiling that made her look like a fancy beekeeper. "*Here* you are, you poor theeng," she shouted. "Steel een this terrible countree. Eet ees pride keeps you here, you know. You weel not admit that you are stranded here and that you hate it!"

That was my moment. They say revenge is a waste of time, but Sybella had driven me too far, and I was determined to fix her red wagon for keeps, for all the mean things she had done and said to me in Paris and on the Riviera. So I only asked her quietly how Tired Charley was.

"Oh, thees American men," she said. "They have no fire, no charm at all. I could not put up with heem any longer."

I noticed she was wearing two new bracelets, and a big, fresh ring, so I figured Tired Charley was a dead pigeon. Probably he had gone back to the butter-and-cheese belt to lick his wounds and work out a way to make money by hand in the basement, thereby replacing the former money he once had before he met Sybella.

She plunked herself down at my table. "All alone," she said. "These Spaniards are so cruel. Never mind, Sybella weel fix theengs once more. I weel show you Spain."

"Not this time, you old parrot," I thought, but did not say anything. When José-Armada came back to the table, and I introduced him to Sybella by his string of titles, she was so surprised three rubies almost fell out of their settings. She recovered though, and said, "Ah, I am so glad my leetle protegée Dorees has one friend, anyhow. I must go now, but I weel call you and see you this evening." She stormed out, her gold veiling at half mast.

José-Armada wanted to know who that was, an aunt of mine? His words filled me with satisfaction. I had been blinded by Sybella's jewels and furs, her gall, and her claims that she knew everyone. I had never even considered that she was old enough to be my aunt, and a not too attractive aunt at that. Confiding in José-Armada, I told him about how Sybella had treated me, and together we planned our revenge.

It worked like a charm. During Sybella's stay in Madrid, I didn't say an unkind word to her. I let her tell me how odd I was looking, I let her criticize my clothes to her heart's content. All I did was introduce her to people. I introduced her, morning, noon, and night to *duques, condes, marqueses*. I took her around and explained places to her, not vice versa. When she would make a blunder, I would be oh so patient, and point out what the right custom was. The people I introduced her to introduced her to their friends. Sybella did not know a soul in Spain whom she hadn't met through me, directly or indirectly. And my Spanish women friends said all the things to her that I wanted to, and didn't dare. She tried to pull the correction routine on them, and it failed with a thud. Spanish women are among the most elegant in the world, and they called Sybella's attention to the fact that her clothes were ghastly colors, that she wore far too much jewelry, that her make-up looked as if she had stolen it from

Bobo the clown, that her voice was easily confused with an alarm bell.

Sybella did not make any headway with the men either. Juan summed it up one night. "That Sybella," he said, "she is so, so ugly, yes?" They wouldn't dream of parting with any money to her, they believed in romance, not barter, the way she did. She would have been lucky to get a bunch of flowers, even.

I believe that Sybella could have stood the lack of loot, if she had been able to point things out to me, and make me feel ignorant. What drove her away were those introductions. She was crushed; she couldn't stand it—simply couldn't stand it. I actually drove her out of town with kindness.

She tried to sneak away from Madrid when she figured I would be out of the hotel. But I had heard the noise of her packing and scolding at the maids the night before, and I was ready for her in front of the Palace when she drove away. "How can you stand eet here?" she wanted to know. "Horrible, thees place. Well, darleeng, the best place for you is a leetle, backward country like thees one. You are not the type for the great, the Paris success. The competition ees too much for you there."

"Spain may be backward to you," I said, "but here they can still tell a pretty girl from a buzz saw."

Sybella tossed her head (thereby loosening her false bun in back), and climbed into her car. She bellowed at the chauffeur, the poodles barked, and they drove away, covered with Spanish dust. I knew that she felt the blow; for once, her plumes were at half-mast. Maybe the bun falling off had disarranged them; anyway, they were sure drooping.

And that was the last I saw of Sybella. I mean the last I have seen of her up to now. I am young yet, and will no doubt travel again. Sybella will still be going strong, I am sure, and my hunch is that our paths will cross once more, perhaps twice or three times more. I still have a tic left from her; when anyone calls me "Darleeng," I start ducking and backing toward the door.

Sybella did take José-Armada's mind off his jealousy for a while. I will say that for her. Heaven knows it was the one good thing she ever did for me, and she didn't even realize it. But once she was gone things started up again, worse than ever. Juan and José-Armada stopped at nothing. They began to tell me awful stories about each other's pasts. If I had believed them, I would have left Spain right then and there. They pulled every dodge of jealousy I had heard of, and a few I hadn't. For instance, when José-Armada heard that Juan had let me stay in a bull ring with a live bull, he pretended to be awfully angry at him. "Why, he reesked your life," José-Armada said, "what an ugly theeng to do. You do not realize what a narrow escape you had." And he insisted on taking me to a bullfight to show me what a narrow escape I had.

It took a lot of persuasion. I didn't want to get in a ring again, even as a spectator. But José-Armada was firm. We went with a party of people, which included a young Swedish boy. He and I became great buddies during the bullfight. We were both torn between awe and nausea. He kept getting sick. I only missed getting sick by a whisker. All that goring and running around, and the bull nearly killing the *torero*. What a sight! The *torero*, I might say, looked kind of like Ricardo. I guess all bullfighters are that way.

He did dedicate a bull to me, though. I got a charge out of that, nausea or no nausea. The bullfighter came and stood under our front row seats and said a lot of Spanish, which I didn't understand. José-Armada told me to stand up. I did, and everyone shouted *"Olé!"* It was better than a movie première. Then José-Armada got the bullfighter to repeat what he said, this time in English. He said that he was dedicating this bull to my beauty, and how he wished it was a braver bull, to be truly worthy of so much beauty. I was flattered, but I was just as glad it wasn't a braver bull. The one he fought looked courageous enough to me.

Afterward, José-Armada insisted that I meet the bullfighter, though I told him I had already met Ricardo, and that I'd had it on bullfighters. If he hadn't seen so ugly, this bullfighter would have made a good impression on me. His speeches were simply beautiful. He asked me to kiss his cheek, and I did, though it took an effort. He then said he would never touch the lipstick print or wipe it away.

That night José-Armada and I saw him in a café, and the lipstick mark was gone. So I went up to his table and said, "I thought you were never going to touch the kiss I gave you." He whipped an embroidered handkerchief out of his pocket, showed me my lipstick on it and said, "Eef I left your leepstick on my cheek, everyone look at eet and see eet there. Here, I weel keep eet forever, and eet weel be mine alone, and no one else's." You can't beat the Spaniards, *duque* or bullfighter. He may have been a country boy, but you would have to get up terribly early in the morning to stay a jump ahead of him.

It was that same evening things came to a head between José-Armada and Juan. José-Armada and I were sitting over some wine after dinner, when Juan stormed in, simply frothing at the mouth. He came right over to us, took off one of the gloves he was wearing, and slapped it across José-Armada's face. "You dog," he shouted. "You peeg, you worthless, you. I weel not have you going out weeth Dorees. She love me."

José-Armada took the glove, and *he* slapped Juan with it. "Peeg yourself," he yelled. "Worm, coward, backstabber. I weel go out weeth Dorees whenever I please, and she weel let me. She love me, not you." He was jumping up and down with rage.

They were standing so close their noses were almost touching and bellowing insults at each other in Spanish too fast for me to follow. I kept trying to tell them that I liked both of them, and wasn't in love with either of them, but they wouldn't stop screaming long enough to listen to me. Even if they had, I don't think they would have believed me. They could only understand *love,* not *like.* Anyway, it wound up with José-Armada saying to Juan, "Eet is a duel. Tomorrow we weel fight. Pistols."

That scared me. All the way back to the hotel, I told José-Armada that he and Juan mustn't do this thing.

It took two hours of talking, and I was hoarse. But he finally agreed that they wouldn't fight, and I went to bed with a peaceful mind.

I will never as long as I live forget my last two weeks in Madrid. In the first place, I got jaundice. I had been feeling queer for some time. One morning I woke up, and I was as yellow as the setting sun. Juan and José both sent their physicians, and they made me stay in bed. I would give parties, yellow in the face, with a red bandanna around my head; I was more Spanish than the Spanish by this time, and so, appropriately enough, with my scarf and face, I looked like the Spanish flag. My titled amigos would flock to my side, and we would play flamenco records and they would tell me how the bullfights had turned out, and who was madly in love with whom.

It was in the middle of one of these parties that I got a bombshell from Junie. I was propped up in bed with the records going, my friends talking, my castanets and bullfighter suit spread out around, my guitar by my elbow, when the maid brought in Junie's letter. She wanted me to come back to America right away. She was getting married! And to the man who owned everything. I cabled her that I would fly back as soon as I could. I kept trying to leave, but every time, somebody would give a party for me, and it would be so marvelous that I would cry and cry and stay on for three more days. This might have continued for years.

But early one morning they called from downstairs to say that I had visitors. I threw on a robe, opened the door, and standing there were two gray-haired ladies, weeping like waterfalls.

"What is it?" I asked.

It turned out that one was Juan's mother and the other was José-Armada's mother. They chorused, "You weel not let thees terrible theeng happen. Say you weel not!" What had happened was that José-Armada had broken his promise to me, and he and Juan were going to fight a duel with pistols after all. I told the old ladies that I would do something. And I did. But to show you how Spain had got hold of me, I hesitated. I felt so Spanish that a duel seemed natural to me. "Why not?" I thought, redraping my mantilla. Then I thought of the kids back home in El Morocco, and in Toots Shor's, and how amazed they would be. My native common sense came to the fore.

I called the plane company; they had a seat left on the afternoon flight to America. I sent two notes, one to José-Armada and one to Juan, telling them it was no use fighting, I was leaving. I packed, and made the plane by two minutes.

The plane landed in Lisbon, where it was to wait for an hour. When I went to get myself something to eat, I heard my name being called over a loudspeaker. I went to the main desk, and there were six telegrams, three from Juan, three from José-Armada. They begged me to come back, they pleaded with me, they swore not to fight. I was tempted, and thought of turning back. But then I thought, no, and got back on the plane.

As I looked down and saw Lisbon getting smaller

and smaller, I knew that I had been right. "There is no use going back to a place," I thought, "if it will only mean that your two favorite millionaires will kill each other." At least this way, both my beaux were alive. And I congratulated myself on my quick thinking.

CHAPTER 8

LONE STAR HOME-COMING

HOME FROM MY TRAVELS, FROM BROADening experiences and new kinds of millionaires, I knew that I was a wiser girl. After all, I thought, there are not so many girls as young as I am who have seen all the domestic brands of millionaires, plus Paris millionaires, millionaires on the Riviera and in Spain...I guess I have seen pretty much of everything.

I was not so blasé that I could turn up my nose at New York however. Even the fierce traffic jams looked good to me, and felt that though I would always love Spain and go back to it, I was an American and a New Yorker, and that those were the places for me. And a New Yorker in a town house at that. Junie, who as I have pointed out before, is not a materialist, still has a sense of true elegance. The town house was no squeezed-up brownstone in a near-slum district. It was gray, near Fifth Avenue, looked kind of like a French chateau, and it must have had thirty rooms to it. As I rang the doorbell, I happened to look up; I noticed a flag with a single star on it, flying from one of the towers. "Some new idea of Junie's," I figured. "Maybe a patriotic gesture to welcome me home. But why wouldn't it be a regular flag then?" Like all of Junie's ideas, I knew I would have to wait and see what it was. Not even I could work them out in advance.

Junie answered the door herself. She got it open only after a lot of tugging and hauling. That ironwork is heavy. After we had yelled our hellos, and cried a little, and she had got the servants to take my luggage upstairs, I looked at her hand. "Junie," I said, "Not already!"

"Yes," she said, "We just couldn't wait. Chaps and I were married a week ago. I wanted to wait until you got here, but I didn't know if you'd even come back for my wedding, you sounded so crazy about Spain."

"Of course I would have," I told her. "But it's all right, in fact it's wonderful. What I want to know is, who in the world is Chaps? I thought this man you loved so madly and who owned everything was named Brandan Millar Schloop III. It's a name you can't forget so quickly."

"Sure his name is Brandan Millar Schloop III, all right," Junie said. "They call him Chaps is all. You couldn't call him all those names all the time."

"No," I said. "Why Chaps? Why not Brandy or Mill or something?"

"Because he's from Texas," Junie said. "Chaps, get it? You know, those kind of leggings the cowboys wear."

"Oh," I said.

"Texans like to refer to their state. It's something dear to them. You'll see," Junie said. "Come on, I'll show you the house."

We began our tour of the first floor. Junie explained to me that the flag was the flag of Texas, the Lone Star State. It seemed a wee bit overenthusiastic to be flying your state flag in New York City, but I set it down to home-town pride that lots of people seem to have. I have never been able to see why. Either live there, or don't bore other people with it, that's what I say. You can be sure I did not express these sentiments to Junie; love, after all, is love, and I felt confident that Junie had married someone fine and worthy of her.

She had chosen all the furniture for the house herself, and I spent hours admiring the pearwood chairs and tables, her antique clocks, marvelous curtains and upholstery, and her mirrors and knicknacks. Everything she had bought was French Provincial; after a while, I couldn't help noticing that someone, undoubtedly Chaps himself, had added a few touches of his very own.

Over a sweet little sofa, covered in off-green and white, there was a size gigantic oil painting of a battle, and through the smoke I could see that the soldiers sure didn't look French, though they did look mighty provincial. "What scene is that?" I asked Junie at last.

"That's the battle of the Alamo," she answered. "Chaps has eleven others, all hand-painted oil paintings, done in Texas, he told me."

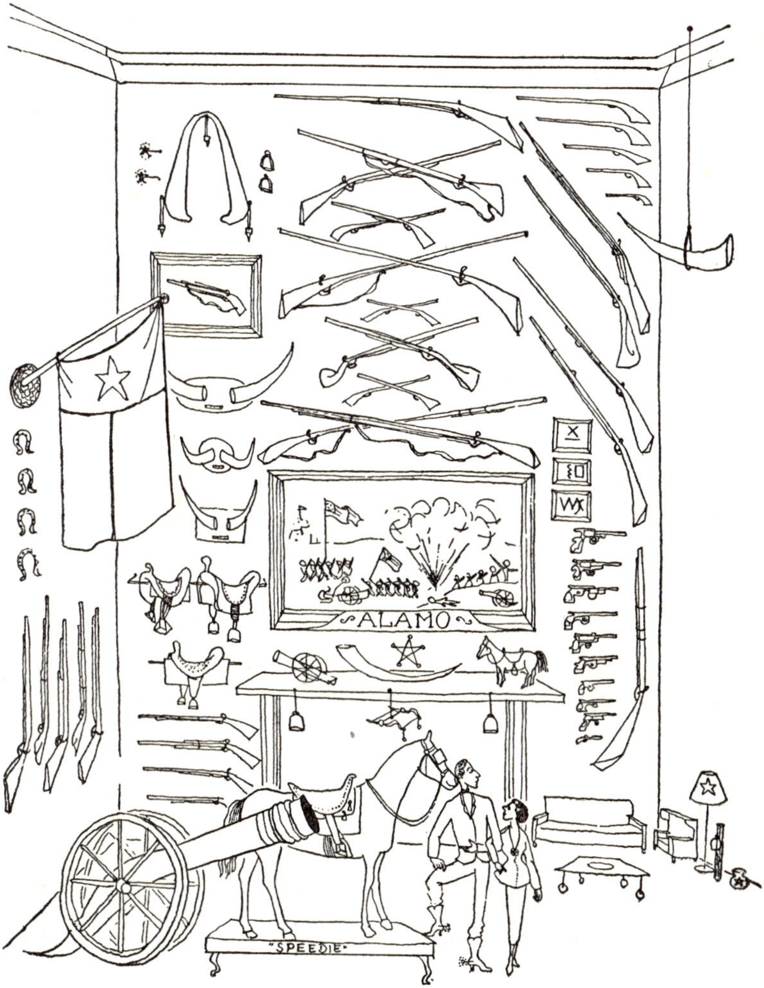

ALAMO
"SPEEDIE"

This was one place, I could see after viewing a few more rooms, where you would be stuck for your own name, before you forgot the Alamo.

Then, I have seen many decorating magazine photographs of genuine old French Provincial houses in France, but I have never seen any spittoons in any of them. In Junie's French Provincial scheme, there were lots of spittoons; brass, each one with a Lone Star engraved on its side. "Not that Chaps uses them," Junie explained. "Hardly at all. It's in memory of his grandfather. He ran a saloon named The Spittoon. Isn't it sweet of Chaps to be so sentimental about his family?"

I agreed, though I couldn't help being happy that Gramps hadn't owned a saloon called the Longhorn Grill, or the Saddle-Up. Without any prompting from Grandpa, Chaps had brought along some longhorns (I couldn't tell from what kind of animal, offhand), and some saddles. These were collected in the gun room. Unlike some gun rooms, this one lived up to its name. It looked quite a bit like an arms and ammunition depot at the height of the last world war. I have never in my life seen so many rifles, revolvers, and pistols under one roof; all of them beautiful imported weapons, in leather coverings. Every piece of leather without exception had the words, Brandan Millar Schloop III, Galosh, Texas, stamped on it.

"See what I mean?" Junie said, "Texans like to be reminded of home." By this time, we were in the doorway of the master bedroom. "Look out you don't bump into the derrick."

"What derrick?" I asked, pausing suddenly.

"Oh it's only a model," Junie said. "See? That's a model of the derrick of the first oil well that came through for Chaps's father."

Model or not, it stood a good seven feet high, and privately, I didn't think it added too much to the bedroom *décor*.

"How many oil wells does he own?" I asked Junie.

After she told me, I looked at the derrick model with different eyes. If oil had done that much for me, I might well have a couple of derricks around, myself. It seemed that Chaps had in the vicinity of five hundred and eighty million dollars in oil, though there were the real-estate firms, silver mines, etc., etc., that Junie had mentioned to me in Paris. His father, or Old Daddy, as Chaps called him, had left him a miserable embarrassing twenty million, which Chaps, through hard work and determination, had parleyed into something respectable.

Junie would have told me more; just then there was a banging and shouting downstairs, and she said, "It's Chaps! He's home!" and started to run to meet him.

"You mean all of that is a single man?" I asked. I think she was too far down to hear me.

I'll certainly say for Chaps, he was one attractive man. Tall, lean, rangy, with a sort of thin, rugged face; something, in other words, out of a Gary Cooper movie. Not something; Gary Cooper. On him the wide brimmed hat, boots, and spurs looked dandy. Though if parquet floors could have talked, I doubt if they would have agreed with me about the boots and spurs. Well, houses are for people, not the other way around, I think. I could see that Chaps agreed with this philosophy; his welcome brought sudden death to two vases. When the echoes had died down some I wondered where he had come from? He said, "The office, ma'am."

Ah, I thought, the first bloom of romance. All this for a day at the office. It turned out that the office was Galosh, Dallas, someplace in Nevada, Seattle, and a few other points north and south. Most men go to the office via train, subway, or Hudson Tube. Chaps went to the office in a reconverted bomber he had bought from government surplus.

"Got to do away with her though," he said, "Too darn slow. Can't get anywhere cruisin' around at three hundred miles an hour." I couldn't make out what he meant by doing away with the plane. Maybe he turned his head to one side and shot it, the way you do with a horse that has a broken leg.

Since I learned that Junie and Chaps were already married, and that I would be the third, or redundant character in the chateau, I had been getting more and more uneasy. Chaps, Junie, and I settled down in the study which boasted three representations of the Alamo: I took the opportunity to make it clear that I would only stay until I had found an apartment for myself. In fact, I said that I would consider it no trouble to take a hotel room that very evening. I was sure the Elchester-Flores would be glad to see me again, with more luggage this time, and more ready cash. Chaps treated my remarks as if I had suggested hauling his gray-haired grandmother off to a cell. I said that anyway I had to get an apartment sometime. Chaps was still outraged; "ma'ams" flew thick and fast. Before I knew what had happened, I had agreed to stay at least two weeks, and to go with them on a hunting trip the coming week end.

"You want to get that stale European air out of your lungs, ma'am, and breathe in some of God's ozone," Chaps said. "And I know you'll like my friend Rovere. I'm goin' to call him now."

While he was on the phone, I asked Junie who Rovere was. "You will be crazy about Rovere Bigelow," Junie said. "He is Chaps's best friend. He looks a lot like Chaps (score three hundred points for Rovere, I thought), and he is so nice."

"All except for his ties," she added. "There is one thing I do not like about Rovere, and that is his ties."

By the time I had unpacked some clothes, bought a few warm things for the trip, and trotted out a few evenings with a beau and Junie and Chaps, it was nearly Friday, and I had a kind of feeling of what a Texas millionaire was like.

It's a double emphasis with him; accent on the millionaire and on the Texas. Without much doubt, Texas millionaires make other kinds look like paupers. Those hundreds of millions are not stuffed into odd investments that will pay off two days before the Last Judgment, or in white elephant mansions, or in obscure corporations, the mean age of whose board of directors is one hundred and fifteen years. No; it's liquid assets; cash, oil, ground; the real, real things. Chaps, like his friends, was generous and forthright. Nothing petty; if he couldn't get the change right away, he'd leave a hundred dollar bill with the taxi driver. When a salesman asked him where he should send the bill for two new cars, Chaps said, "Send it to Brandan Millar Schloop III, Texas, U.S.A. It'll get to me." And it did.

The other part is Texas. Whatever or whoever the Texas millionaire loves, Texas is first, the person or thing second. One night I just happened to be humming, "Home on the Range" under my breath while shuffling cards for a game of bridge. I glanced at Chaps, and the tears were standing in his eyes. Had "Deep in the Heart of Texas" still been popular, he would no doubt have stood at rigid attention until I stopped humming. The Texas millionaire sticks to what he learned in Texas. What's good there is good in New York. The Thursday night before we were to go to Maine, Chaps, Junie, a café society type man, and I were in El Morocco, eating dinner. The waiter asked us what we would like for dessert. Chaps repeated what we all wanted; what he wanted and asked for was pie à la mode (à la mode as in Alamo. Maybe that was the connection). The waiter's eyebrows drew down over his nose, my café society playmate tried to look as much like a banquette as possible, and I studied the floor. Even Junie looked a little numb. But it was pie à la mode back in Galosh, and it will be pie à la mode wherever he may be, just like he will never trade in his wide brimmed hat for a Homburg.

Friday morning bright and early, Rovere Bigelow arrived, or maybe I should say, exploded. He and Chaps hollered and hallooed and gave each other ringing clouts on the back. I wouldn't swear to it, but I thought I heard them fire a couple of shots, not in anger, naturally, just in the flush of the moment.

I was on to the Texan indifference to space limitations, so I greeted the news that Rovere had flown in from London, where he had passed three days, with calm. I asked him how he liked London.

"Confinin', ma'am," he said.

Rovere really did look like Chaps; tall, rangy, and so on. Rovere was breezier looking, however. He always appeared to be caught in a high wind: the brim of his hat curled up on one side, his shirt was a trifle twisted, and his tie was unfailingly over his shoulder. Happening to be in back of him, I got a peek at the tie itself, and was glad for the gale. It was a green number, hand painted with pictures of nude women, sticking their toes in bathtubs. That's the only kind of tie Rovere seemed to own; different colors maybe, but always those nude women. Sometimes they were dancing, sometimes they were playing harps. One was kind of like an old Greek theme; on that one they were weaving at looms.

I kept waiting for Chaps and Junie to come out with Rovere's nickname, hoping that it might develop that it was "Oil." No; they went right on calling him Rovere.

While we were standing alone at the foot of the stairs, ready to get into Chaps's car, I asked him about it. "How come they call you Rovere and never anything else," I asked. "Isn't that kind of fancy for Texas's taste?"

"No, ma'am," he said, "it isn't. Not a-tall. It's the name of the town I was born in. Rovere, Texas. And I wouldn't think of shortenin' it, because I swear by that little old town."

Which explained all.

On the surface of it, our trip to Maine seemed simple and well organized. As I understood it, Junie, Chaps,

Rovere, and I were to fly up in Chaps's seaplane, and stay at Chaps's hunting lodge. However, complications had set in. Chaps had gone to a cocktail party the Wednesday before. Junie had been overseeing some painters who were doing the kitchen, so she hadn't gone with him, or it would never have happened. On his own, in a burst of unrestrained enthusiasm (and a few drinks, as Chaps admitted), he had asked a third of the cocktail party to come along too. Most of them had accepted. It took all three of Chaps's town cars to get us, the guns and ammunition out to New Jersey where the two seaplanes were. (Rovere had donated his to the cause of sociability.)

The four of us were piled in one plane, together with the hunting equipment. After a lot of sputtering and talk, it developed that we couldn't go by seaplane after all. Chaps had brought along so many guns and so much ammunition that the seaplane couldn't even get off the water. We had to traipse over to an airport and take the ex-bomber to Maine.

In Maine, we were met by three limousines, two for the guests and one for the guns and ammunition. For a minute, we thought it was going to have to be the other way around; but the men finally got the stuff jammed into one car.

Chaps's "hunting lodge," as I had suspected, turned out to be a newly built old Southern mansion, with enough space in it so that Republicans and Democrats alike could have held conventions there, without getting into arguments. They would never have seen each other.

We assembled in one of the drawing rooms for cocktails before dinner, and I got my first good look at the cocktail party salvagings. My heart sank when I thought of those characters out in the woods, loaded down with loaded rifles. "It will be murder," I thought.

I was comforted by the thought that the men looked as if they couldn't bear to let go of a glass long enough to grab a gun, and also the thought that the women, if they shot at anything, looked as if they were planning to pick each other off. I am not overly selfish; but, having barely escaped being gored by a Spanish bull, I was not wild with enthusiasm about being drilled by a shaky blonde. I did not sleep very well that night.

Abercrombie and Fitch would have blushed to see the group we made next morning. The cocktail males favored a "Dawn and Fireworks over Manhattan" theme... the plaids that blind. Some of the girls were all set in high heels and Fifth Avenue *tailleurs;* all of them looked stunned by the fresh air which they had not breathed in so long. One of them seemed to have bought up the costumes from *Annie Get Your Gun* at theatrical auction; she was one mass of fringed buckskin.

Chaps passed out the weapons; the cocktail contingent set off, crashing and thrashing into the underbrush. After they were out of earshot, he said, "Well, let them have fun. Rovere here and I are goin' to do some honest, Texas-style shootin'. How about you and Junie-honey?" Junie had no desire to shoot anything, and I was too scared of bagging one of the plaid set, so we said we would merely walk along with Chaps and Rovere while they hunted.

Six hours later (with time out for sandwiches), neither of them had fired a shot; Junie and I were half dead with exhaustion and burning feet. We had seen a lot of game; birds and deer. Rovere and Chaps would have nothing to do with it. As Rovere put it, "We aren't goin' to fire a shot at anything that isn't worthy of a Texas sportsman." I wondered what they expected in Maine; tigers? Anyway, on we walked, scrambling around rocks and gullies, hot and bothered, our coiffures in shambles, our faces shinier than brand new pennies. Chaps and Rovere in the late afternoon decided to separate. We stayed with Chaps, hoping that since he was the host, he would take the initiative and shoot something worthy, so we could go home and put our feet in an Epsom Salts bath.

We crept along for another half hour, and had about given up seeing the house again when Chaps stiffened, raised his gun. We heard a noise in the bushes, heard a "Bam," and an animal cry. "You got it!" Junie shouted, "What is it?"

It was Rovere, with a nasty wound in the arm, pitched over on the ground, his tie with the weaving nude woman still resting on his shoulder. He bore no grudge, even made a joke of it. "One Texan is always worthy of another Texan's bullet," he said.

Junie and I stayed with poor Rovere while Chaps went back to the house and got some help to carry him in. A local doctor extracted the bullet. I flew to New York with Rovere, and saw him bedded in a hospital.

When I got to the town house, there was a message from a South American friend of mine to phone him.

I did, and he said he was going back to South America, giving up his apartment. Would I like it? I saw it, it was lovely, and I took it. By the time Junie and Chaps had returned, I had signed the lease and packed my bags. I explained to them that I had to move right in, as I had already paid a month's rent. They understood, and waved me good-by for a while, standing on their doorstep, the Lone Star flag floating above their heads.

I knew I could have stayed on with them, and I also knew that Rovere wanted to see much more of me. That he had told me on the way to the hospital. Yet I couldn't quite throw myself into it. After all, I had my health, and what good are barrels of oil if you are a bullet-riddled sieve?

It took an awful lot of work, but by night Junie and I had the apartment pretty well fixed up. Though there was still luggage all over the place, my books were in the bookshelves, my pictures were hanging on the walls, and my kitchen equipment was piled in the kitchen cupboards.

We were resting, drinking cokes as usual, when Junie said to me, "You know, Doris, I like being married real well. It's relaxing. Why don't you give it a try yourself?"

I thought for a while, and drank more of my coke, and told her, "Well, Junie, I have always promised myself that I wouldn't settle down till I had seen every type of millionaire in every place there is. Look at Rovere for instance. When I got back from Europe I thought I'd seen them all, and I hadn't even met the most outstanding kind, a Texas millionaire. Who knows? There are probably lots of other kinds I don't know either. I haven't been to England, or Sweden, or China, or Louisville, Kentucky. No, Junie, I think I will wait."

"Maybe you are wise," Junie said, "if that is your goal. The only reason I am happy with Chaps is because I love him."

I got us two more cokes, and we sat and thought some more.

"We sure have met a lot of millionaires," Junie said. "I wonder how we did it?"

"Gee, pigeon," I said, "I don't really know. Except that we dressed up real nice and opened our eyes to new vistas."

"We did," Junie said, "and we were strong. We had the strength, and we were lucky too."

"You are so right," I told her, "I guess that's the way with everything. I guess that's how to meet a millionaire, all right. Look pretty, keep an open mind, be lucky, and you can go right on meeting them for a long, long time."